Early American
Decorating Techniques

Early American Decorating Techniques

Step-by-Step Directions for Mastering Traditional Crafts

Mariette Paine Slayton

THE MACMILLAN COMPANY / *New York, New York*

COLLIER-MACMILLAN LIMITED / *London*

Photographs from *The Ornamented Chair*, *The Ornamented Tray*,
and *The Decorator* are used through the courtesy of the
Historical Society of Early American Decoration, Inc. (HSEAD, Inc.)

The Macmillan Company
866 Third Avenue, New York, N. Y. 10022
Collier-Macmillan Canada Ltd., Toronto, Ontario

Library of Congress Catalog Card Number: 75–180297

FIRST PRINTING

Printed in the United States of America

ACKNOWLEDGMENTS

MY FIRST EXPRESSION OF GRATITUDE goes to my husband for his moral support as well as for his technical advice about painting materials. I am also indebted to Mrs. Raymond McCandless for typing the manuscript and doing such a masterful job of editing; to Mr. and Mrs. Robert Keegan who read the manuscript and offered many helpful suggestions; and to Walter Wright and Mrs. Sherwood Martin, in whose classes I improved techniques and obtained a number of teaching ideas. My appreciation, also, for the kindness of my fellow teachers who so willingly lent me originals and patterns from their collections.

I wish that credit could be given individually to the many students in my classes who generously shared their innovative ideas, both academic and otherwise, who brought in original pieces to be recorded, and who constantly expressed interest and enthusiasm. To all of them, warmest thanks for making my teaching years so pleasurable.

COLOR ILLUSTRATIONS

PLATE 1   *Color wheel, and colors used in country painting (Facing Page 4)*

PLATE 2   *Color chart of ten basic colors used in Early American decorating (Facing Page 5)*

PLATE 3   *Steps in painting country-tin flowers or fruit (Facing Page 20)*

PLATE 4   *Applying bronze powders to varnish (Facing Page 21)*

PLATE 5   *Applying the stencil (Facing Page 68)*

PLATE 6   *Floated color on stencils and painted foliage (Facing Page 69)*

PLATE 7   *Typical freehand-bronze units (Facing Page 84)*

PLATE 8   *Etching on metal leaf (Facing Page 85)*

PLATE 9   *Colors and mixtures used in Chippendale painting (Facing Page 164)*

PLATE 10   *Step-by-step paintings of Chippendale-type flowers (Facing Page 165)*

PLATE 11   *Step-by-step paintings of three types of Chippendale roses (Facing Page 180)*

PLATE 12   *Typical lace-edge flowers, leaf, and border designs (Facing Page 181)*

CONTENTS

Acknowledgments v
List of Color Illustrations vi
Introduction xi

PART ONE / LEARNING THE TECHNIQUES

    I · Country Painting 3

        PAINTING THE BASIC STROKES 7
        PAINTING DOTS 10
        PAINTING BASE COATS 10

    II · Color and Additional Painting Techniques 14

        COLOR WHEEL 14
        MATCHING COLORS BY ANALYSIS 15
        COLOR CHART 16
        STEMS AND VEINS 17
        SQUIGGLES OR CURLEYCUES 17
        TRANSPARENT OVERSTROKES 18
        FLOATING COLOR 19
        BLENDING TWO WET COLORS 20
        BLENDING COLORS WITH THE FINGER 20
        COPYING A PATTERN 20
        MOUNTING AND STORING PATTERNS 22

    III · Stenciling 23

        STENCILING WITH BRONZE POWDERS ON TIN AND
          WOOD 27
        STENCILING AND PAINTING ON VELVET 35
        WALL STENCILING 42

    IV · Freehand Bronze 47

        EXECUTING THE DESIGN 48
        SOLID UNITS 48

SHADED UNITS   49
USING A BOB AND STUMP   51
USING A BRUSH   52

V · *Gold Leaf*   *53*

PICKING THE PROPER SIZE   57
PAINTING THE DESIGN   57
APPLYING THE LEAF   58
STENCILING WITH GOLD LEAF   59
MAKING REPAIRS ON GOLD LEAF   60
ETCHING   60
SHADING WITH PAINT   61
STORMONT, FINE LINES, AND SQUIGGLES   61
APPLYING GOLD LEAF TO IRREGULAR SURFACES   62

VI · *Chippendale Painting*   *64*

MODELING WITH LIGHT AND SHADE   65
PAINTING CHIPPENDALE FLOWERS   67
PRELIMINARY EXERCISES IN PAINTING   68
STEP-BY-STEP FLOWER PAINTING   70

VII · *Lace-Edge Painting*   *77*

STROKE EXERCISES FOR LACE-EDGE PAINTING   80
PAINTING LACE-EDGE FLOWERS AND LEAVES   80

PART TWO / APPLYING THE TECHNIQUES

VIII · *Preparation of Tin and Wood*   *85*

RESTORING ANTIQUE TIN   88
NEW TIN   91
WOOD   91
OPAQUE BACKGROUNDS   91
TRANSPARENT BACKGROUNDS   92
SMOKED BACKGROUNDS   93
BRONZED BACKGROUNDS   94
TORTOISE-SHELL BACKGROUNDS   94
ROSEWOOD GRAINING   95
TONGUE-OF-FLAME GRAINING   95
STALE-ALE OR PUTTY GRAINING   95

IX · *Applying the Decoration*   *97*

PAINTING POSITIONS   98
WHITE BANDS   98

Gold Bands   100
Transferring the Tracing to an Article   100
Mother-of-Pearl Inlay   101
Striping   102

X · *Finishing*   *105*

Varnishing   106
Handrubbing   109
Other Finishes   109
Antiquing   109
Alcohol-Proof Finish   111
Weatherproof Finish   111

XI · *Reverse Painting on Glass*   *112*

Stenciling on Glass   113
Gold Leaf on Glass   115
Painting on Glass   119
Repairing Original Glasses   121
Tinsel Painting   122

XII · *Problems and Solutions*   *125*

Country Painting (Chapter I)   125
Color and Additional Painting Techniques
    (Chapter II)   126
Stenciling (Chapter III)   126
Freehand Bronze (Chapter IV)   127
Gold Leaf (Chapter V)   128
Chippendale Painting (Chapter VI)   128
Lace-Edge Painting (Chapter VII)   129
Preparation of Tin and Wood (Chapter VIII)   130
Applying the Decoration (Chapter IX)   130
Finishing (Chapter X)   131
Reverse Painting on Glass (Chapter XI)   132

Part Three / Patterns

Full-Size Patterns of Early American Designs   *135*

Epilogue   *233*

Appendix   234
    SUPPLIES AND EQUIPMENT   234
    SUPPLIERS   237

Bibliography   240

Index   243

INTRODUCTION

EARLY AMERICAN decorating is the art of restoring and reproducing the stenciled and painted decoration found on antique furniture, tinware, and glass, as well as on walls and floors. At one time the craft was referred to as "tray painting," but that term was even less inclusive. Actually, anything from an English snuffer tray to a large Chinese screen can be restored or reproduced by Early American decoration.

This art, in which interest is increasing along with the general upswing in artistic activity, is becoming one of the most popular crafts. This may be due to the fact that no special creative talent is needed and the many techniques involved provide a limitless range of uses. This book is presented as a course of study, working from simple beginning processes to the more complex and advanced so that it can be used as an individual text for those who are unable to attend a class. It might also be helpful to the amateur craftsman who wishes to improve his work or to the teacher of classes in art or art education.

Any instruction book must, by its very nature, be clear, concise, and to the point. The only drawback in such a style is, of course, the absence of the human warmth and presence of a good and encouraging teacher. As I think back and remember my own teachers, one in particular comes to mind, whose amusing but pertinent homilies I pass on with the hope of offering encouragement in moments of frustration or slow progress.

Mr. William Crowell was my first teacher, and I feel it was a rare privilege to have studied with him. He was an old-time craftsman who was largely self-taught through the restoration of old decorated pieces which came his way. His formal education was limited but, as he often reminded us, he had "sat at the feet of Frank Mathewson for six months learning the art of painting on canvas," and he preferred to be known as a painter rather than a decorator. His father was a fine cabinetmaker and undoubtedly he received inspiration and some training from him.

His teaching methods were highly haphazard, and after a few lessons many a beginner (with delight and some surprise) would take home a large painted tray complete with birds, flowers, and a fountain. Some of us felt that we were not learning much, as we depended on him for constant guidance; but nonetheless a number of his more serious students went on to fruitful careers in teaching and custom decorating.

However, we were all convinced—rightly or wrongly—that we were in the presence of a true authority on all artistic processes. "Ain't nothin' to it," was his usual comment when confronted with some mystery of the craft brought to his attention by a perplexed student. He would then go on to give a complete analysis of the process with related experiences and anecdotes.

Cries for help would invariably bring the comforting assurance that "there's no trouble you get into that you can't get out of." While this approach built up much-needed confidence for us, it occasionally resulted in watching the complete dissolution of our artistic effort in a turpentine bath. On the other hand, overconfidence that seemed to be threatening his authority was handled with the admonition, "When you think you're good, you're done," thus keeping our personal dreams of glory within bounds, and artistic goals out front.

His basic messages, when reviewed in retrospect, held good advice for the beginner—have no fear of new challenges, don't get discouraged when you make mistakes, and never reach the point where you are not willing to learn. If this simple counsel is kept in mind, a beginner should have no great problems, but rather a new and satisfying adventure in artistic expression.

PART ONE

LEARNING THE

TECHNIQUES

I

Country Painting

COUNTRY PAINTING is not the earliest form of decorative painting but is essentially an American art form that was used on household tinware shortly before 1800. These gaily painted articles were a refreshing change for the housewife who had been using somber pewter and wood in her kitchen. Now almost any piece of decorated metal—antique or reproduction—is loosely referred to as "toleware," but this is a misnomer since "tole" is actually a French word meaning "sheet iron." *Tole peinte*, or "painted iron," refers to early French decorated metal articles.

One of the earliest producers of household tinware was Edward Pattison who moved with his brother from Ireland to Berlin, Connecticut, in 1740. When decoration became popular, many of the Berlin women were pressed into service and, according to the records, were paid two dollars a week. It is interesting to note that these records show that although labor was cheap, materials were not. Even then, brushes cost a dollar each and the best varnish sold for ten dollars a quart! Peddlers who sold the articles traveled into many states and sometimes as far as Canada.

Country painting is found on many different types of articles, such as trays, boxes, tea and coffee pots, cannisters, candleholders, etc. The treatment of the basic designs varies according to areas so that the locality, and sometimes the decorator, of many of the articles can be identified. Some of the more famous names of decorators are Zachariah Stevens and Oliver Buckley, both of Maine; Oliver Filley of Connecticut; and Ann Butler of New York.

3]

SUPPLIES AND EQUIPMENT

Brushes (Figure 8) A *scroller*, or *liner*, is a long-pointed brush which is useful for painting long, thin lines such as veins, stems, swirls, etc. A *long-pointed quill* can also be used for similar strokes. A *Finepoint brush* is a short, red sable watercolor brush which has an exceptionally fine point. Any similar brush of another make would be adequate.

The *bright's brush* is a square-tipped; short-hair; black-, red-sable, or bristle brush. Since it is used primarily for canvas painting, it has a long handle which can be cut to a length convenient for your purposes.

A brush which is almost "all-purpose" is the Fashion Design Quill made by Winsor & Newton. Someone once called it the "mink coat of brushes," and unfortunately its rising cost seems to justify this definition. The pointed quills are mounted on handles and come in proportioned lengths (No. 2 is ¾ inch). They are a real delight to use and are worth experimenting with. They are available wherever Winsor & Newton supplies are sold.

Cleaning Brushes It is important to keep brushes clean and in good condition, not only because it is impossible to do good work with a brush that is in bad shape, but also because many are expensive to replace. For *temporary* cleaning (while the brush is in use), clean the bristles with turpentine before using another color. For *permanent* cleaning (when putting your project aside for a period of time), clean the brushes in turpentine as before. Then when all color has disappeared, dip them into Energine or cleaning fluid (always replace the cap quickly, as the fumes are harmful). Lastly, wipe the brushes and dip them into lard oil or Vaseline hair tonic. Point up the pointed brushes and flatten out the square-tipped ones, leaving enough oil in the brush to keep it soft. Brush cleaners such as Silicol or Kem (KemTone Products) can also be used.

If a brush has not been properly cleaned and the paint has hardened in the heel, soak it in brush cleaner or paint remover until the paint has softened. Then wipe carefully and wash in soap and water, rubbing the heel against a cake of soap (Ivory or Fels Naptha) until all the paint particles are removed. Rinse, shape, and set aside to dry. It is not a good idea to go through this process too often because it tends to take the life out of the brush.

Storing Brushes Keep your brushes in a brush box which has wire coils to hold them in place, tape them to cardboard, or stand them in a can or jar. Never store brushes where the tips will be hitting any surface which will curve the bristles. If this should happen, dip the brush in *hot* water, shape, and allow to dry.

Artists' Oil Colors For decorative painting, oil paints can be purchased in small 3½-inch tubes. I suggest that you buy artists' oil colors in order to avoid getting the poorer quality type that is used for tinting prepared colors. There are many good

[*4*

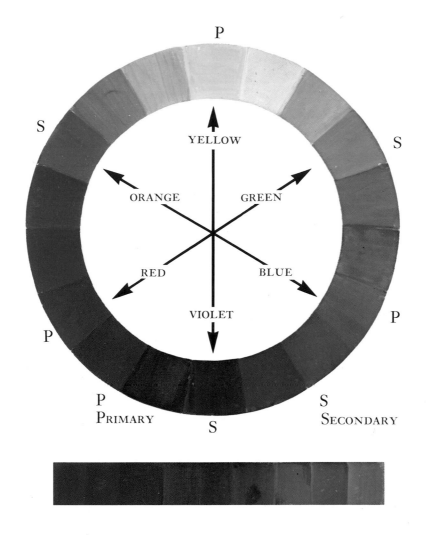

P

S   S

YELLOW

ORANGE   GREEN

RED   BLUE

VIOLET

S   P

P

P PRIMARY   S   S SECONDARY

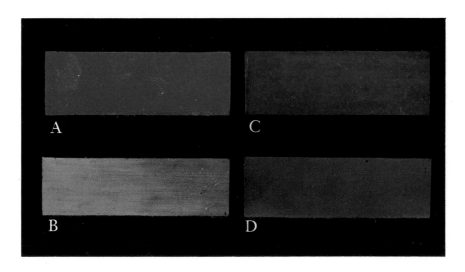

PLATE 1 *Top:* color wheel. *Center:* two complementary colors mixed in graduated quantities to produce a neutral color at the center. *Bottom:* colors used in country painting: (A) cadmium red, light (oil color), or orange-red in japan; (B) chrome yellow, medium, in japan and burnt umber painted from opaque to semitransparent; (C) chrome yellow medium, Prussian blue, and raw umber; (D) striping white in japan, Prussian blue, and raw umber.

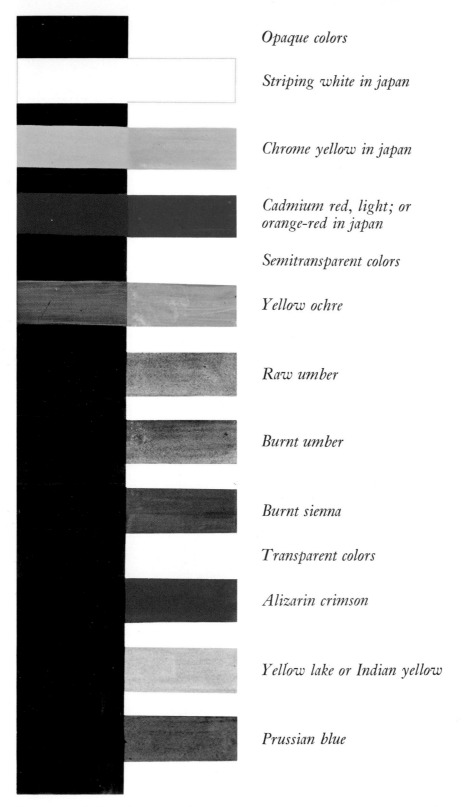

Opaque colors

Striping white in japan

Chrome yellow in japan

Cadmium red, light; or
orange-red in japan

Semitransparent colors

Yellow ochre

Raw umber

Burnt umber

Burnt sienna

Transparent colors

Alizarin crimson

Yellow lake or Indian yellow

Prussian blue

PLATE 2 Color chart showing the ten basic colors used in Early American decorating. Opaque colors cover both black and white backgrounds. Semitransparent colors cover white and show faintly on black. Transparent colors cover white but are invisible on black.

brands of paint, such as Winsor & Newton, Grumbacher, Craftint, and Weber. But unfortunately all brands do not produce the same shades in all colors; some are less opaque or less transparent than others. Most brands of yellow ochre are satisfactory. Craftint's cadmium red, light, seems to be the best orange-red in oil color and the most opaque. English vermillion is a good color, but it has become too expensive. Unless you can find a yellow lake (oil paint with a translucent pigment) which is truly transparent, a satisfactory choice is Weber's Indian yellow. Different brands of Prussian blue and alizarin crimson differ slightly, but not enough to make it necessary to stick to one brand.

Japan Colors Japan colors, or colors ground in japan oil, differ from artists' oil colors in that they have better covering qualities and dry faster. Although they come in a number of colors, it is especially helpful to use them in the opaque colors. Ronan's Signcraft red (in cans only) and King Cole medium orange seem to be excellent colors for country-tin reds.

Tubes of japan paint should be shaken well before using; otherwise much of the oil will squeeze out when the tube is opened. Tubes should be stored upside down to allow the oil to rise to the bottom. If the paint seems to be hardening, cut off the tube's bottom, squeeze the paint into a small jar, and add enough turpentine to cover; this will keep it soft. When you wish to use the paint, remove it from the jar with a palette knife.

Varnish When varnish is used as a medium to mix with paint, it must be light and fairly slow drying. Pratt & Lambert's No. 61 Clear Gloss is a generally popular brand. If this is not available, experiment with another brand, such as Man of War Varnish, Master Mixed Spar Varnish (Sears Roebuck & Company), or Watson Standard's No. 44 Floor Varnish. Some decorators use Nobles & Hoare's Quick-Drying Gold Size.

Storing Varnish When varnish is not used up within a short period of time, a skin forms over the top and the varnish eventually becomes thick, jellylike, and impossible to work with. Although a little turpentine can be added to the varnish when it is being used as a *painting medium*, it is much better to try to prevent or at least to delay this action by proper storage. There are several ways of doing this. If the varnish is left in the can, the cover must be replaced tightly after each opening by, for example, hammering it in place or stepping on it. Another way to keep varnish in usable condition is to leave the cover in place and punch two holes in the bottom of the can for pouring. Screws or wooden golf tees can be inserted in the holes after each use. Varnish can also be stored in long-necked bottles, such as those used for Tabasco and Worcestershire sauce, or in wine bottles for larger amounts. After using, breathe into the bottle before replacing the cap and then carefully tip the bottle once or twice. The carbon dioxide in the breath replaces the oxygen in the bottle and tends to delay the formation of a skin.

Palettes   A regular artist's wooden palette is all right to use, but a paper palette requires no cleaning. Vegetable parchment, which can be bought by the pound at creameries, can also be used; it is less expensive than paper palettes, but it should be weighted so that it does not slip while you are mixing paints. Some people use heavy, shiny pages from magazines, but the print is sometimes distracting.

Paint Rags   Old sheets or any thin cotton material that is not linty make good paint rags. Paper towels are better than facial tissue.

Black Paper and Cardboard   Black paper and cardboard are usually available at art stores which carry decorating supplies. The cardboard is glossy black on one side and white on the other. Two brand names are Duragloss and Plasti-Sheen. Another lightweight cardboard, which is black on both sides and less glossy than these, is called Kroydon Cover; it is available at Rourke-Eno Paper Company in Hartford, Connecticut. One brand of black paper is Hazenkote.

Worktables   A worktable should be firm with a smooth top. When applying background paints to articles, protect the tabletop with newspapers. For any other operation, a plain paper is better. Ask at your paint store for old rolls of wallpaper which are to be discarded. This can be cut to the proper length and tacked or taped to the table, figure-side down.

Chippendale tray (reproduction). Gold-leaf scrolls, and painted flowers and birds. Painted by Cornelia Keegan. [From The Ornamented Tray]

Chippendale tray (reproduction). Bronzed background; gold leaf and painting. Painted by Helen Hague. [*From* The Ornamented Tray]

PAINTING THE BASIC STROKES

BECAUSE the strokes involved in country painting serve as a foundation for all the other techniques described in this book, a mastery of these strokes is very desirable for the beginner in Early American decoration. Perseverance in practicing country-painting strokes will make all the other techniques except stenciling much easier.

The seven basic brush strokes (Figure 1) will be referred to as (1) BROAD; (2) KNIFE; (3) TEARDROP; (4) STRAIGHT; (5) OVAL; (6) S; and (7) CRESCENT. They are all painted with a square-tipped, No. 3 quill. This is an extremely versatile brush that can be used in different sizes to produce many of the strokes found in Early American decorating designs.

1. Squeeze a dab of oil paint about the size of a pea onto your palette. Pour some varnish into a small glass or metal container and some turpentine into a larger one. Bottle caps can be used for the varnish; but if they have a plastic lining, remove it before using the caps.

2. Pick up a square-tipped quill which has been mounted on a wooden handle. To prevent the handle from slipping out of the quill, dip it in Elmer's Glue before inserting it, and then allow it to dry. If the brush has been moistened in oil to keep it

7]

FIGURE I *The seven basic brush strokes:*
(1) broad; (2) knife; (3) teardrop; (4)
straight; (5) oval; (6) S; and (7) crescent.

soft, clean it in turpentine before using. After cleaning, dip the brush first into the varnish and then into the paint. Dress the brush (i.e., wipe it back and forth on the palette) until the mixture of paint and varnish is evenly distributed throughout the bristles and any excess is wiped off. The brush should now be quite flat, with a sharp-edged, or knife, tip.

[*8*

3. Holding the brush on the practice paper so that the wide edge touches the paper, draw the brush toward you to make the BROAD STROKE (Figure 1).

4. Shift the brush so that the knife edge is pointed toward you and only the corner is touching the paper, and make the KNIFE STROKE (Figure 1).

5. For the TEARDROP STROKE (Figure 2), hold the brush in the second position (as in Step 4), and press or push it to one side; then gradually draw it toward you in an arc, slowly raising it to a perpendicular position. Do not twist the brush but let

FIGURE 2 *Positions of hand and brush when painting a teardrop stroke.*

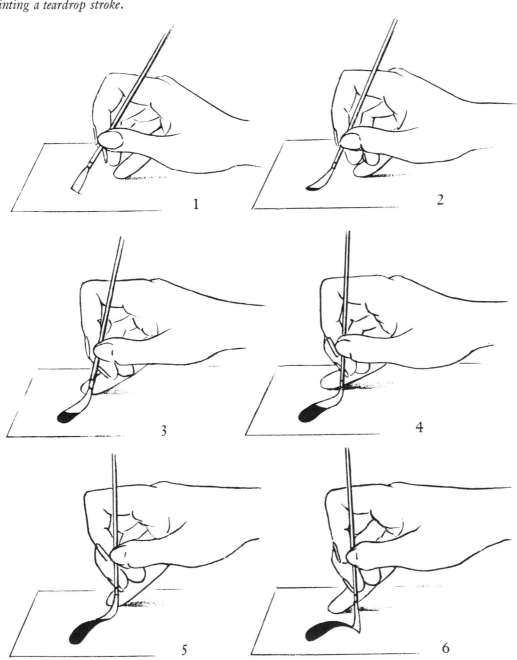

the bristles fall naturally into the knife shape to paint the fine tail. Grasp the brush in a way that is comfortable for you and that allows the greatest ease of manipulation. The hand should be just off the table, supported by either the little finger or the other hand.

6. The STRAIGHT STROKE (Figure 1) is made with the brush in the same starting position as that used for the teardrop stroke; however, instead of pushing the brush to one side, push it straight down and gradually draw it toward you in a straight line, raising it to a perpendicular position for the fine tail.

7. The OVAL STROKE (Figure 1), unlike the last two, has a point at the beginning and end. At the start hold the brush in the knife-edged position, but instead of pushing down or pressing it to one side to get a rounded tip, pull very slightly and then start pressing down to get the desired width. Gradually let the brush up to finish with a point.

8. The S STROKE (Figure 1) also has a point or fine line at the beginning and end. The first, or squared-off, example is simply to show the directions for the narrow and broad strokes. Notice that the two fine lines which are painted with the knife edge are parallel, and the broad stroke is perpendicular to them. Be sure to bring the brush up to a more perpendicular position when moving from the broad into the knife stroke.

9. The CRESCENT STROKE (Figure 1) has points at the beginning and end. Start with the knife edge and gradually press down as you bring it around in an arc; then gradually raise the brush and finish the stroke on the knife edge.

PAINTING DOTS

1. Load the square-tipped brush with a rather soupy mixture of paint and varnish; dress only enough to mix the two together, but not enough to wipe off any excess.

2. Use the corner of the square tip to paint the dots. The size will depend on the amount of mixture and the pressure used. Dots can also be made by dipping a stylus (or any tool with a small, rounded tip) into a paint-and-varnish mixture and touching the spot. For convenience, hold a palette knife with some of the mixture close to the area being painted.

PAINTING BASE COATS

BASE COATS are the first layers of paint on a design. When they have thoroughly dried, transparent washes of color and/or transparent overstrokes are applied. To get the best results, base coats should be painted with a minimum of strokes. Find out just what your brush can do and you will save yourself time and frustration later on. Let the brush do the work for you. Outlining and filling in is not only a waste of time, but it will never produce the clean, sharp edges and smooth surfaces that are the hallmark of an experienced decorator.

Victorian-shaped tray with elaborate scrolls on border, and flowers in natural colors. Owned *by Mr. and Mrs. Stanley Paddock. [From* The Ornamented Tray]

After acquiring some skill in painting the basic strokes, try the exercise in Figure 3; this shows the combinations of basic strokes that can be used to paint the base coats for fruit, flowers, and leaves. Use the same paint-and-varnish mixture and paint on practice paper. Eventually you will be able to look at the design you wish to copy and immediately recognize which brush strokes were used and also which combinations will produce the necessary base-coat shapes.

When you have gained some confidence in handling the brush, start working on a black background, as in Figure 4. This shows both correct (A, B, and C) and incorrect (D, E, F, and G) strokes. In D not enough varnish was used in the mixture, so it is dry, with a feathered edge. Too much varnish was used in E, so the edges crept. In F the stroke was started with the broad instead of the knife edge. The hook in G resulted from pushing the brush to one side and letting up slightly before finishing the stroke.

Since the majority of country-tin designs were painted on black or dark backgrounds, it is necessary to know something about the consistencies of the paint mixtures. The traditional yellow brush strokes on original tin pieces varied from opaque, when no background shows through, to almost transparent—when the background shows through and seems to change the color. Probably the most effective stroke is one somewhere between opaque and transparent that results in a fairly

11]

FIGURE 3   *Combining basic strokes to paint*
base coats for fruit (1), flowers (2 and 3),
and leaves (4, 5, and 6).

transparent tail which gives the stroke the illusion of form. The base coats were usually orange-red and very smooth and opaque.

Apply base coats in the following manner:

1. Load the square-tipped quill as you would for a brush stroke. Make two crescent strokes to outline the shape and fill in with broad strokes.

FIGURE 4 *Strokes painted on black background in varying degrees of transparency.* A, B, *and* C *represent correct strokes;* D, E, F, *and* G, *incorrect strokes.*

2. Flatten the tip of your brush either with your fingers or by pressing the heel of the brush on the palette to spread the bristles. The square tip should be made as wide as possible. Stroke the painted base coat very lightly across the strokes until no brush marks show. This is not always easy, as there must be enough paint in the mixture to cover the background but also enough varnish so that the mixture will flow together without ridges. If necessary, paint two thin layers, letting the first one dry before applying the second. Be sure that the paint does not build up on the edges.

II

Color and Additional Painting Techniques

THE OBJECTIVE OF the serious student of Early American decoration is to faith-fully reproduce designs or copies of designs found on decorated antiques. The careful reproduction of the old designs is a valuable contribution to historical research in the field of decoration and most students try to achieve a high level of accuracy and authenticity. However, once the old techniques are learned, they may be varied and given new application to satisfy creative students.

In reproducing the old patterns, matching the colors is a primary requirement. Although there is no necessity for an in-depth treatment of color theory, reproducing colors will be much simpler if you become familiar with the properties of color and the color wheel, which is the key to all color mixing.

COLOR WHEEL

ALL COLORS have three properties: HUE—is it blue? . . . green? . . . yellow? INTENSITY, or CHROMA—is it a *bright* blue or a *dull* blue? VALUE—is it a *light* blue or a *dark* blue?

Study the color wheel in Plate 1 and note the following:

1. The three primary colors are red, yellow, and blue; from these primary colors other colors can be made.

2. The three secondary colors are orange, green, and violet. These are made by mixing two *adjacent* primary colors: orange can be made by mixing red and yellow; green by mixing blue and yellow; and violet by mixing red and blue.

3. The complement of each color is directly opposite it on the color wheel. A

[14

color can be grayed or dulled by adding its complement. Theoretically, then, when equal amounts of two complementary colors are mixed in the center of the wheel, a gray or neutral color is produced.

MATCHING COLORS BY ANALYSIS

IN ORDER to match a color, first analyze its hue, intensity, and value. Next pick a tube color which comes closest to its hue.

HUE: Hue can be changed in two directions by adding either of its two adjacent colors. Thus red can be changed to orange-red by adding yellow, or to violet-red by adding blue. Yellow can be changed to green-yellow by adding blue, or to orange yellow by adding red; blue can be changed to green-blue by adding yellow; or to violet-blue by adding red.

INTENSITY: Generally intensity can be changed by adding the complementary color (directly opposite on the color wheel) or by adding white, gray, or black. In decoration we usually substitute raw umber and burnt umber for gray and black. Another general rule is to use raw umber with cool colors—blues and greens—to keep them cool; and burnt umber with warm colors—reds and yellows—to keep them warm.

VALUE: Value can be changed from a medium to a light tone by adding white; these are called *tints*. Value can be changed from medium to dark by adding black or

Sandwich-edge tray with Chippendale painting and gold-leaf scrolls on partially bronzed back- *ground. Owned by Mrs. John Ames. [From* The Ornamented Tray]

one of the umbers; these are called *shades*. You will notice that on the color wheel the colors have different values. Yellow is the lightest, and violet is one of the darkest. Therefore, some of the primary and secondary colors can be used to darken colors. In our limited palette, alizarin crimson and Prussian blue are the darkest values.

Let us assume that you feel fairly familiar with the color information above. Your thoughts when analyzing and matching a color may run something like this:

"These strokes are orange-red (hue), dull (intensity), and a medium shade (value). I will use cadmium red, light, which is a medium orange-red, and add a little burnt umber to tone down the intensity."

Or like this:

"This flower is a light (value), dull (intensity) blue (hue). I will start with white because it is a tint, add Prussian blue to get the right hue and value, and add some raw umber to cut the intensity."

As you become more experienced in mixing colors, you will be no more conscious of these thoughts than a musician is of individual notes when reading music.

COLOR CHART

THE CHART in Plate 2 will help you to become familiar with the ten colors you will be using. The first three are called opaque colors. This means that you cannot see through them as you can through colored glass; therefore they have a good covering quality, and cover black areas as well as white. The next four are called *semitransparent*. You can see through these colors and they do not cover black well; but they become more colorful when painted over a white background. The next three are *transparent* colors, which are almost invisible on the black background but which look brilliant when painted over white. Transparent colors must be used over a light background or mixed with white in order to show their true colors.

Black is not included in the list of paints because it is ordinarily used only for strokes, veins, etc. For these, use black enamel or seal, which is described in Chapter IV.

The four mixtures shown on Plate 1 are colors which, with occasional variations, are used in country painting. When mixing colors on your palette, always use a palette knife. A brush could be ruined if used often for this purpose. As a general rule, do not mix a large puddle of paint and varnish on your palette for use in loading the brush. Varnish dries more quickly than oil paint and unless the mixture is used up fairly quickly, it might become too sticky to flow well. The exception to this rule would be in the use of japan colors, when side-loading the brush (Chapter III), or when striping (Chapter IX). Japan colors dry faster than varnish so the addition of a little varnish prevents them from hardening.

SUPPLIES AND EQUIPMENT

Pens Tracings done in ink are much more durable and easier to see than those done in pencil. Crow-quill pens can be bought with a holder. These pens produce a very fine line and should be used with black drawing ink (India ink). Tracing pens, which are like fountain pens with a tracing point, are easy to use; but they are rather expensive, somewhat temperamental, and need to be cleaned regularly. As a precaution against damage, it is a good idea to place a tiny piece of damp sponge in the cover which goes over the point.

Tracing Paper Tracing paper comes in rolls and pads of many different sizes. Quality differs slightly; it is best to get the kind that is the most transparent.

Supersee Supersee, or frosted acetate, is a semitransparent paper which is shiny on one side and dull on the other. It comes in different weights, but No. 3 (.003 inch) is the one generally used for this work. Some decorators prefer to paint on clear acetate, which is absolutely transparent. This obviates the necessity for varnishing the pattern before mounting but the shiny surface is more difficult to paint on, especially for beginners. Both kinds of acetate can be bought at stores which carry decorating supplies.

Table Easel Table easels can be bought, but small ones which are adequate for all but very large patterns can be made with heavy cardboard and masking tape (see Figure 6).

STEMS AND VEINS

1. Use a No. 2 scroller and load the brush as previously explained. Instead of flattening it on the palette, roll it back and forth to get a good point.
2. Holding the brush in a nearly perpendicular position, pull it along the guideline and exert more pressure at any spot where the line widens. Veins should be done freehand. Start the center vein at the base of the leaf and the side veins at the center. It is sometimes easier to stand up to do long, thin strokes.

SQUIGGLES, OR CURLEYCUES (FIGURE 5)

1. Use a No. 2 Finepoint brush and a fairly soupy mixture of paint and varnish. Roll the brush to a good point.
2. Hold the brush in an absolutely perpendicular position, supporting your hand with the little finger or by resting it on your other hand. Try to keep an even pressure as you paint the squiggle.

17]

FIGURE 5 *Designs showing how various strokes can be combined. Also shown are a* squiggle, or curleycue (top center) *and leaf veins.*

TRANSPARENT OVERSTROKES (PLATE 3)

OVERSTROKES of a semitransparent red and white are found on many country-tin designs. They are always added *after the base coat is dry.* The red is a mixture of alizarin crimson, burnt umber, and varnish; the white strokes are made

[*18*

ABOVE: *Pictorial tray with gold leaf border.
Owned by Audrey Dunn Franz.*
[*From* The Ornamented Tray]

with striping white in japan and varnish. Paint the strokes as you would any brush stroke, but keep them thin enough for the background to show through. Dress the brush well so that the strokes will not spread at the edges.

FLOATING COLOR (PLATE 3)

OCCASIONALLY a round red or yellow flower or fruit design will have a light and/or dark transparent wash of color—called a floating color—on one or both sides. The dark areas correspond to shadows and the light area to highlights so that the shape appears to have form. Here's how to achieve that effect:

1. With a square-tipped quill, paint clear varnish over the entire base coat. (Be sure the base coat is completely dry before applying the varnish.)

2. Load the same brush with the desired color and paint a fairly heavy stroke on one side of the base coat.

3. Quickly clean the brush in turpentine and dip it in the varnish. Dress the brush on the palette, pressing at the heel of the brush so that the tip becomes quite wide.

4. With a very light touch, stroke the surface where the painted stroke meets the clear varnish area. At first keep the strokes going in the same direction as the original color stroke; but if the result is streaky, try crossing the strokes. Keep stroking until the overstroke color has worked into the clear varnish and no line

19]

appears where the color stops and the base coat begins. This must be done quickly because as soon as the varnish begins to "set up" (get sticky) it cannot be worked. To slow the drying a bit, you can add a drop of linseed oil to the varnish when you start to use it.

BLENDING TWO WET COLORS (PLATE 3)

A FEW country-tin designs that originated in the Maine area include motifs in which two colors are blended while the paint is wet:

1. Paint the two colors so that the edges touch. Keep the paint mixture fairly dry—do not use too much varnish.

2. With the square-tipped quill which has been cleaned and dressed to produce a broad tip, or with a *dry* bright's red-sable brush, lightly stroke the edge where the two colors meet until one blends into the other with no visible line.

BLENDING COLORS WITH THE FINGER (PLATE 3)

IN PENNSYLVANIA German designs, blending is very often done with a patting technique:

1. The base coat must be dry. Load a square-tipped quill with the shading color. Use a little less varnish than that used for floating color. Paint a broad, rather heavy stroke on the side of the base coat.

2. With your finger, lightly pat the area where the color ends and the base coat starts; pat until there is no line of demarcation between the two.

COPYING A PATTERN

1. Lay a piece of tracing paper over the tracing of a pattern or painted pattern, and attach with masking tape.

2. Trace the outlines with a medium-soft pencil or pen and ink.

3. When the tracing is finished, remove the paper and tape it to a piece of card-board or heavy paper.

4. Place a piece of clear or frosted acetate (Supersee) over the tracing and secure it with tape. If frosted acetate is used, paint on the dull side.

5. Place the pattern you are copying in front of you on a table easel (Figure 6). Now you are ready to paint the pattern on the acetate, following the tracing lines on the pattern underneath. Always paint the base coats first—that is, those areas which will receive the overstrokes after the base coat is dry.

If you find it difficult to work on parts of the pattern while some of the paint is still wet, make a *bridge* (Figure 7) by taping a piece of artgum eraser, about ½ inch thick, at both ends of a 12-inch ruler. Lay the bridge on the pattern, making sure that the erasers do not touch the wet areas, and rest your hand on the outer edge of the bridge while you paint.

6. As soon as all the tracing areas have been painted on the acetate, slip a piece

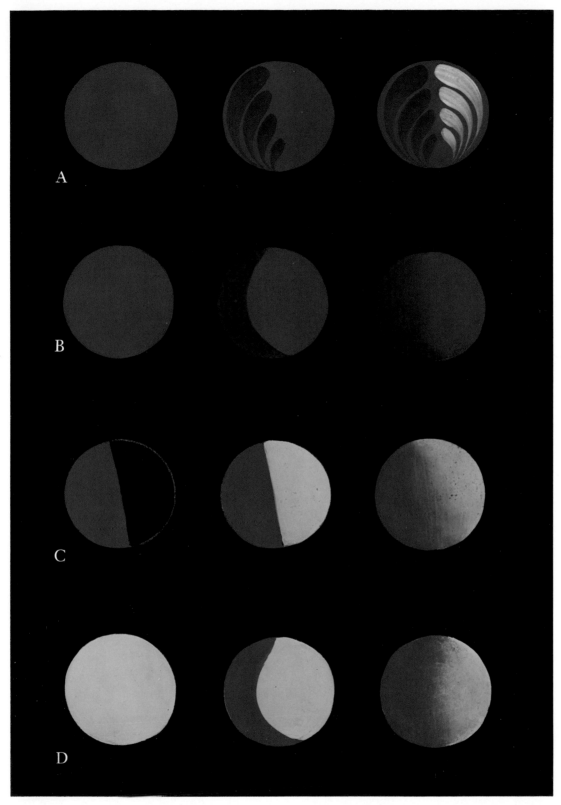

PLATE 3 Four treatments, in three steps each, of the country-tin flower or fruit: (A) orange-red base coat with overlays of thin alizarin crimson, and white teardrop strokes when dry; (B) orange-red base coat with floated color; (C) orange-red and yellow blended while wet; (D) yellow base coat with orange-red patted on when dry.

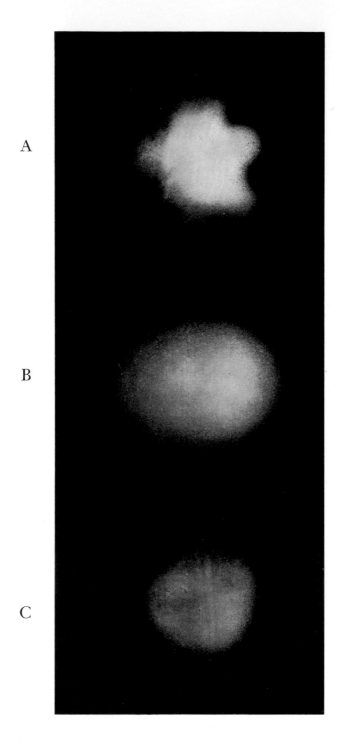

A

B

C

PLATE 4 The successful application of bronze powders to an article is dependent upon the tackiness of the varnish. In A the varnish is too wet; the shading changes abruptly from light to dark. In B the tack is right, and the powder blends easily and gradually. C illustrates varnish that is too dry; if a line shows on the edge of the stencil, much of the powder disappears when it is washed with soap and water.

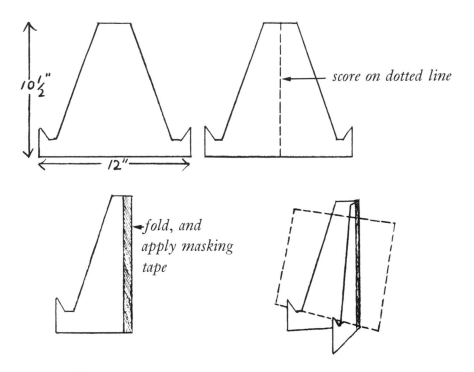

10½"

12"

score on dotted line

fold, and
apply masking
tape

FIGURE 6   *Diagram for making a table easel
from heavy cardboard.*

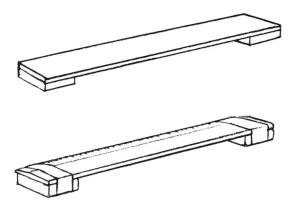

FIGURE 7   ABOVE: *bridge made from wood
scraps.* BELOW: *bridge made from a ruler and
artgum erasers.*

of paper that is the color of the desired background—most often black for country
tin—between the tracing and the painting, and continue with the finishing overstrokes, color washes, etc. It becomes much easier to match colors when you are
painting on the same color as that in the pattern. If the design of the overstrokes is
too complicated to do freehand, trace it on the dried base coat, as explained in
Chapter IX.

7. If your pattern has been painted on frosted acetate, give it a coat of varnish
after it has dried. This eliminates the frosted quality and lets the background color
show through more clearly.

21]

Chinese scene in gold leaf and bronze powders on black background. [*From* The Ornamented Tray]

MOUNTING AND STORING PATTERNS

PATTERNS CAN BE mounted and catalogued so that they may be easily located when you want to use them:

1. Cut a piece of paper the shape and color of the article or pattern you have copied, and mount it on a piece of cardboard with rubber cement. It is a good idea to keep the cardboards nearly uniform in size for each group of patterns.

2. Lay the painted pattern in place over the mounted background-shape paper, and either staple or tape it to the cardboard.

3. Lay a piece of clear acetate over the pattern and tape it to the cardboard at top and bottom.

4. Attach an index tab at the top. Mark each mounted pattern with a category and number.

Small patterns can be stored in boxes or display books that have clear acetate double pages. These display books can be obtained from office supply and photography stores. Large patterns can be stored in sketch portfolios or loose-leaf binders which are available in several sizes at art supply or stationery stores. It is wise to keep a separate list and description of each pattern, particularly if you acquire a large collection. Then, in case one of the numbers is missing, you will know which pattern to look for.

III

Stenciling

APPLICATION OF A DECORATION through sections cut from paper or metal is called stenciling. For centuries stencils have been used with paints and metal powders to create decorative designs. In its highest form, stenciling can rival the artistry of free-hand painting; in the hands of an unskilled craftsman, the repetitious and some-times crude designs earn little praise. The somewhat mechanical character of the techniques makes it appear deceptively simple, but the number and variety of ways in which it has been used over the years have required skill and imagination.

Some of the finest examples of early stenciling come from Japan. Oriental craftsmen cut incredibly delicate stencils, some of which had hairs or silk threads separating the sections. The stencils were used with both fabric and paper, and it is thought that the bronze-powder stenciling being reproduced today had its origin in Oriental lacquer work. Europeans also made use of stencils in their own forms of decoration. French and English stenciled wallpapers imported by colonial Americans became the inspiration for the stenciled walls which aroused the interest of anti-quarians and interior decorators thirty or forty years ago.

The golden age of stenciling in America came in the early years of the nine-teenth century when this type of decoration was applied to velvet and walls, and the more familiar bronze-powder stenciling was used on tin and wood. During this period decorated tinware became so popular that a quicker method of decorating was needed to increase production. The earlier gold decoration had been painstakingly painted with a varnish-type medium; when it was tacky, or almost dry, the metal-leaf or bronze powders were applied. The substitution of stencils which could be

23]

used over and over made it possible to produce thousands of trays and other decorated pieces each year.

Extremely lovely effects were achieved in some of the early work by using many single stencils to build up a composite design. The pictorial designs depicted all sorts of subjects—from the first steam train, to a Bengal tiger about to pounce on its victim. Washes of transparent color were often used to give more realism to the scenes. In some of the later stencil decoration, when the craft was beginning to deteriorate, one-piece stencils were used and the bronze powders (which included colored powders) were crudely applied.

Stenciling, alone or combined with other techniques, is found most often on rectangular trays, but occasionally it was used on small sharp-edged Chippendales and even on coffin trays which ordinarily carry country-tin designs. It was also used extensively in the decoration of various types of furniture, including chairs, benches, chests, beds, tables, and pianos. Probably the most familiar of these is the Hitchcock chair which was produced in Connecticut between 1812 and 1853 with many variations. Early originals bear the inscription "L. Hitchcock, Hitchcocksville, Connecticut, Warranted"; on the later versions the name of Hitchcock's partner, Alford, was added.

SUPPLIES AND EQUIPMENT

Template   A template is usually a metal or plastic sheet. Graduated sizes of different shapes, such as ovals and circles, have been cut into the metal or plastic, and these holes, or negative shapes, form the template. Available at art supply stores.

Stencil Knives   An X-acto knife with a No. 11 blade seems to be a popular tool for cutting stencils. Some people prefer a No. 16. Others use a single-edged razor blade or a surgical knife. The blade must be kept sharp. To sharpen, moisten the blade with light oil or water and press it at an angle on a carborundum whetstone. Move the blade around in an elliptical motion. Turn it over and sharpen the other side.

Stencil Scissors   Stencil scissors must have very fine and very pointed blades. The best ones are well worth the investment if you are going to do much stencil cutting.

Magnifying Glasses   Some of the more complicated stencils require such fine cutting that it is almost impossible to do a good job without using some sort of magnifying glass. There are several kinds: one is balanced against the chest; another looks like motorcycle goggles; still another is free-standing with a flexible gooseneck; and for the person with glasses, there is a clip-on type.

Punches   A dentist's rubber dam punch can sometimes be acquired from a dentist who no longer uses it, or it can be bought at a dental supply house. Leather punches can be purchased where craft supplies are sold.

ABOVE: *Papier-mâché snuffer tray decorated in two shades of gold leaf.* BELOW: *Metal box and tray with country painting.* [*From* The Ornamented Tray]

Architects' Linen   Architects' linen is a fine cloth which has been treated so that it is almost like stiff paper. It is either a light blue or white, dull on one side and glossy on the other. Available where decorating supplies are sold.

Stencil Paper   This is a tough, semitransparent paper which is useful for stenciling on velvet or walls because it does not slip as much as the linen. It is not practical to use for designs with very fine cutting, however. Available in 18 by 24 inch sheets from Sanford Ink Company, Bellwood, Illinois.

Varnish   See Chapter X, page 105.

Varnish Brush   The brush used for applying varnish can be either the one described in Chapter X, page 106, or the background brush described in Chapter VIII, page 88. A new substitute for a varnish brush which has appeared recently on the market is called a *poly brush*. It is actually a bevelled piece of sponge rubber attached to a handle. Although I have not experimented with it extensively, I find that it lays a bubble-free coat of varnish on cardboard. To clean, swish it in turpentine, press with a paper towel twice, and wash in soap and water. These so-called brushes are very inexpensive, but probably will not last very long.

Velvet and Chamois   The kind of silk velvet needed for stenciling is very hard to find. The best samples come from people's attics. The velvet that is on the market is usually synthetic and the pile is too coarse. Experiment with whatever you find, and if none is satisfactory, a piece of soft chamois will be an adequate substitute.

25]

Bronze Powders   Always buy lining powders for stenciling. They come in many different colors under a variety of names or numbers. The four mentioned in the supply list will cover your needs in the beginning. (See Figure 14.) Rich gold is a fairly bright greenish gold which is used more than the others. Deep gold should be more of an orangey-gold and deeper than the rich gold. It could be called a number of names in different brands, so it would be well to select the bronze powder by color. Fire powder is a red color which turns to orange when varnished. It might be helpful to make a chart of the various colors for use in matching whatever color you are working from.

Palette (Figure 14)   To make a palette for your bronze powders, cut a piece of cardboard about 6 inches square and score it down the middle so that it can be folded. Cover it with velvet or velveteen that overlaps the edges, and tape the edges on the back with masking tape. Sprinkle rows of lining powder on the velvet across the fold, leaving at least an inch between rows. Fold the palette and hold together with a clip or elastic band. The palette can be made without the cardboard by folding the velvet, then rolling it up and securing it with an elastic band, but the powders do not stay in place quite so well.

Bright's Sable or Bristle Brush   See Chapter I, page 4.

Contact Paper   This paper is actually a lightweight cardboard with an adhesive on one side. The sticky, adhesive side is covered with waxy paper. Contact paper is sold by the yard, and can be ordered from Shopsin Paper Company, 92 Vandam Street, New York, New York 10013.

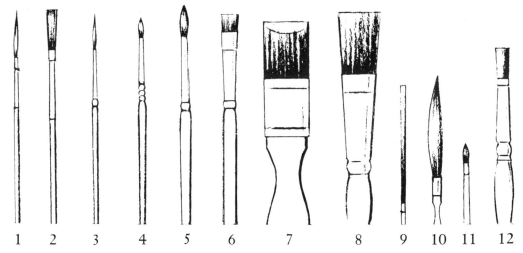

1   2   3   4   5   6   7   8   9   10 11 12

FIGURE 8   *Brushes required in Early American decorating: (1) long-pointed quill; (2) ¾-inch square-tipped quill; (3) scroller, or liner; (4) Finepoint (pointed red-sable watercolor brush); (5) the Spotter (red-sable watercolor brush); (6) red-sable bright's brush; (7) varnish brush; (8) stroke brush used for backgrounds; (9) rattail striping quill; (10) sword, or dagger, striper; (11) short-pointed quill; and (12) bristle stencil brush.*

Stencil Brush   The stencil brush has round bristles that are flat on the top. It is always held perpendicular to the work so that the flat top hits the surface of the work.

STENCILING WITH BRONZE POWDERS ON TIN AND WOOD

BRONZE POWDERS are made from metal alloys, and will tarnish in time. Baer (O. A. Both Corporation) uses combinations of zinc and copper. Aluminum is used for some of the silver shades. The variety of shades produced is determined by the proportions of the metals used and by the grind of these metals. The coarser powders are more brilliant than the finer ground, or lining, powders. When mixed with or rubbed into a tacky or almost-dry varnish medium, bronze powders have the appearance of gold and silver; in all likelihood they were originally used as substitutes for the more costly gold and silver leaf.

To be more fully effective, stenciling with bronze powders must be done on a dark background, so most stenciled articles are painted black, dark shades of color, or in imitation wood grain.

Stencils can be cut on architects' linen or on bond paper which has been oiled or shellacked. Most people prefer the former. The cutting must be done carefully, following the outline exactly, for poor cutting will show up when the stencil is applied to the dark background. Some people prefer to use only a knife for cutting; others use only scissors. Both tools seem to be useful for different types of cutting (Figure 9).

TRACING THE STENCIL

1. Lay a piece of architects' linen, dull side up, over the design and tape in place.
2. Trace the outlines of the design, preferably in ink. When tracing a number of single units on one piece of linen, be sure to allow at least 2 inches between units so that when they are cut apart there will be at least a 1-inch margin around each unit. Templates can be used to true up tracings of circles and ovals.

CUTTING THE STENCIL

1. Cover the edges of an 8 by 10 inch piece of glass with masking tape. Lay the linen, shiny side up (the tracing is less distracting on this side) on the glass and slip a piece of black paper or cardboard under the glass. The black paper sometimes makes it easier to judge the quality of your cutting.
2. If cutting is done with an X-acto knife, be sure that the blade is sharp. Holding the knife at about a 45-degree angle and using a fair amount of pressure, cut along the tracing lines. Always cut the smallest areas first, and try to keep curved lines rounded and points sharp. Single lines such as veins in leaves can be cut more efficiently by using both knife and scissors. No matter how fine the line is, cut down one

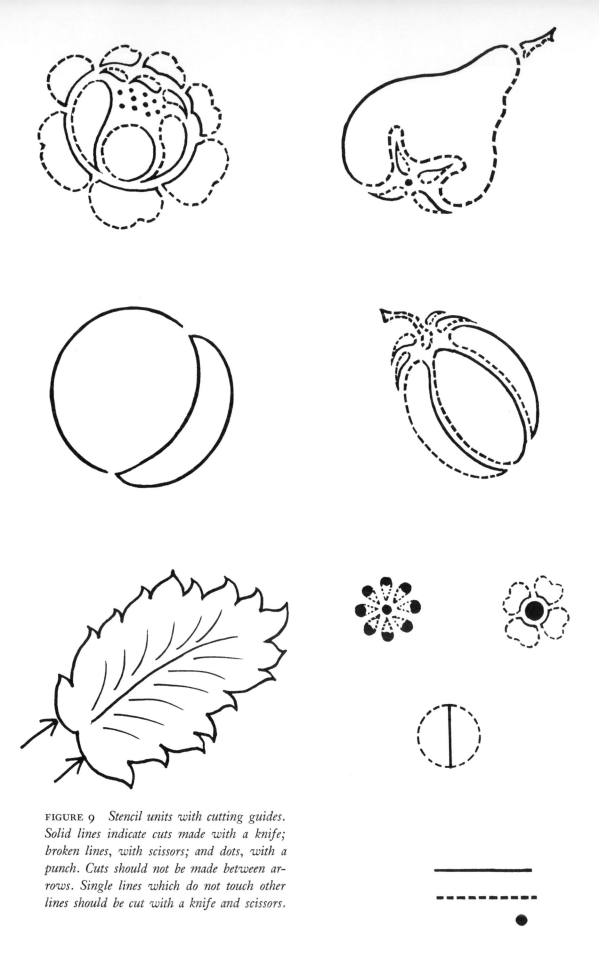

FIGURE 9 *Stencil units with cutting guides.*
Solid lines indicate cuts made with a knife;
broken lines, with scissors; and dots, with a
punch. Cuts should not be made between ar-
rows. Single lines which do not touch other
lines should be cut with a knife and scissors.

side with the knife and back on the other side with the scissors. The width of the line can be more effectively gauged when using the scissors, which are easier to control.

3. Use a dentist's rubber dam punch for punching small holes and a leather punch for larger holes. Punch the holes last.

4. When the stencil cutting is completed, carefully press the stencil on both sides with a warm—not hot—iron. If a steam iron is used, be sure that there is no water in the iron, as water will ruin architects' linen. Pressing is important because it flattens the stencil as well as any edges that might have been bent in cutting.

MENDING A STENCIL

1. If the knife accidentally cuts into a place which should not be cut or if a stencil gets torn, cut two small pieces of Scotch tape and press one on each side of the cut.

2. Recut any open area which has been covered by the tape.

CLEANING AND STORING STENCILS

After using a stencil, clean all the bronze powder from both sides with turpentine or cleaning fluid. Always store stencils flat. They can be kept between the pages of a scrapbook or in manila envelopes. Small stencils can be put into sandwich bags before they are placed in the manila envelope.

APPLYING THE STENCIL

Bronze powders are most effective when used on black backgrounds. Occasionally a one-piece stencil is used on a light-color background, but if there is any shading involved, the area behind the stencil units must first be painted black and allowed to dry before applying the varnish for stenciling.

1. Paint a thin coat of varnish on a piece of black cardboard or black paper. See Chapter X for varnishing directions. If the paper is used, it should be taped to a piece of cardboard to keep it from shifting while work is being done. Set the cardboard aside where there is a minimum of dust. A quick method of making impressions of your stencil is to varnish the black cardboard, using a piece of nylon stocking in place of a brush. The varnish will set up almost immediately. This method, however, is satisfactory only for making impressions, checking for errors, or for future copying. It would be impossible to produce quality stenciling on this background.

2. If you are stenciling directly on an article, prepare the article with background paint as explained in Chapter VIII. Flat black paint is sometimes quite absorbent and the first coat of varnish painted over this black paint dries unevenly. For this reason, before applying the varnish for stenciling it is better to prepare the article by first applying one coat of varnish, allowing it to dry, and then rubbing it with No. 0000 steel wool. Then proceed as you did for making a pattern.

ABOVE: *Oval tray with gold-leaf and freehand-bronze decoration. Owned by Margaret Willey.* BELOW: *Oval handhole tray and* *metal box with country painting.* [*From* The Ornamented Tray]

3. After forty-five minutes to an hour—depending on the kind of varnish used and the weather—test the tackiness by pressing the corner of a piece of architects' linen, glossy side down, on a spot near the edge. If the linen can be lifted off with only a slight pull, and there is no mark left on the varnish, the article is probably ready for stenciling. A word of caution, though: edges, such as the flange of a tray, seem to dry a little faster than flat surfaces; therefore, even if this part is ready, the floor of the tray might still be too wet.

4. When the tack is right (Plate 4), lay the stencil, glossy side down, on the varnished surface in the proper position and press the edges down. When a composite stencil with many small units is being reproduced, it is helpful to make a key stencil which is applied first. This is a piece of linen the size of the complete design on which a large central unit and very tiny portions of other units are cut in their proper relationship. When stenciling the key cutouts, be sure to stencil only the edge of anything that is shaded. Solid units can be done solid. When this key is removed, the other units can be placed wherever their keys have been stenciled. Another method for locating the proper placement of single units in a composite stencil is to first trace the design on tracing paper, then place this tracing over the article and slip the stencil into its proper position under the tracing and over the piece that is being worked.

[*30*

Remove the tracing and stencil the unit. The tracing can sometimes be taped on an edge of the article and flipped back and forth as needed.

5. Wrap a piece of soft chamois or silk velvet around your index finger and twist it so that it will stay in place. Be sure there is an area on the ball of the finger with no folds (Figure 10).

6. Dip the ball of the covered finger into some bronze powder on your palette and rub around on an extra piece of paper to remove any excess powder. Very little powder is needed. When you need to pick up more powder, before going back to the palette, rub your finger in the excess powder that you rubbed on the paper. (Some stencilers rub the powdered finger on the back of the other hand to remove the excess powder, but this practice may be questionable from a health standpoint.)

7. Place the powdered area of the finger on the highlight area of the design, and using a fair amount of pressure, move the finger in a rotary motion to polish the highlight.

8. When the highlight is bright enough, *gradually* lessen the pressure and bend the finger back so that the part of the velvet which has picked up the least powder is doing the work. Work out from the highlight, still using a rotary motion, and continue to lessen the pressure so that the light area blends into the black background with no line of demarcation between light and dark (Plate 5).

9. When the varnish is dry—in about twenty-four hours—wash the stenciled design with mild soap and water to remove the loose powder. Spots of excess powder can be rubbed out with a damp cloth and Lava soap. Rinse and dry.

1. Lay square of velvet or chamois over extended index finger.

2. Fold back away from thumb.

3. Twist tightly away from thumb, and hold in place with thumb and middle finger.

FIGURE 10   *Using a chamois or silk velvet "finger" to apply bronze powders.*

NEGATIVE OR SILHOUETTE STENCIL (Plate 5)

This process is the reverse of the one just described in which stenciling is done only through openings cut in linen. In negative stenciling, the shape which has been cut out is laid on the tacky surface and the stenciling done also from the edge out, producing a black design against a silver or gold background. It is often used in the corners of stenciled border designs. The blending of the powder from the edge of the stencil out until it disappears into the background is referred to as BLOOMING.

SHADING WITH A BRUSH (Figure 11)

Although a better polish is obtained by using chamois or velvet, a short-pointed quill can be used for shading. After polishing the highlight and shading off slightly, pick up some bronze powder with the quill brush and tap off the excess on a piece of paper. Using the side of the brush, start in the highlight area, and with a rotary motion gradually blend the powder until it disappears into the background.

FIGURE 11 *Using a short-pointed quill for shading bronze powders.*

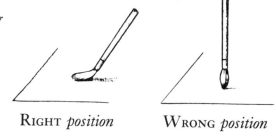

RIGHT *position*   WRONG *position*

USING TWO COLORS

When a unit is stenciled in bronze powders of more than one color, blend off a bit beyond the highlight area with the first shade. Cover your finger with a clean piece of velvet or, if working with a brush, use a clean one. *Starting with the highlight area*, blend the second color gradually into the background, as in Step 8.

FLOATING THE COLOR (Plate 6)

Floating transparent reds, blues, greens, etc., over the stenciled design is much more effective than using colored powders, which are usually coarse and lose much of their color when varnished.

1. Be sure that the stenciled pattern or article is well washed and dried. Apply a coat of varnish and allow to dry for at least twenty-four hours. This protective coat of varnish will make it possible to wipe off mistakes in the color and repaint without affecting the stencil underneath.

2. If the area is to be done in one solid color, dip a No. 5 square-tipped quill

into varnish (pick up a fair amount) and then into the transparent paint. Dress the brush on the paper palette until the desired shade is obtained. (The less mixture left in the brush, the lighter the shades.) Then paint over the stencil, using as few strokes as possible. Don't worry about going over the edge, as the transparent color should not show on the black background. If the paint looks streaky, widen the tip of the brush by pressing the heel on the palette and stroke lightly across the streaks until the paint flows together.

3. If the area is to be colored in shades ranging from deep to pale, first paint the entire area with clear varnish. Immediately mix some transparent paint with varnish on the brush, dress it, and paint a rather heavy stroke on the design where the deeper color shows. Quickly clean the brush, then dip it into clear varnish, and either flatten the brush on the palette or spread the tip by wiping it with the fingers. Lightly stroke the edge of the dark area in the same direction as the painted stroke until the line between the dark and light color disappears.

Round papier-mâché tray with overall gold-leaf and freehand-bronze decoration. Owned *by HSEAD, Inc. [From* The Ornamented Tray]

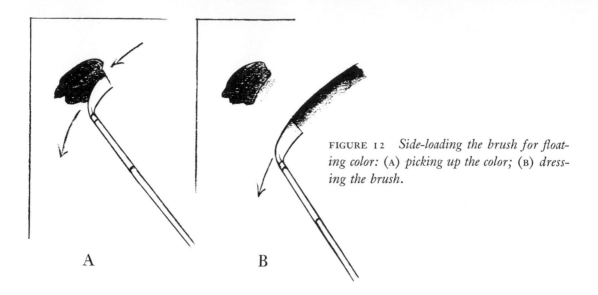

FIGURE 12 *Side-loading the brush for float-ing color:* (A) *picking up the color;* (B) *dress-ing the brush.*

A   B

FLOATING COLOR WITH SIDE-LOADED BRUSH (Figure 12)

Another method of floating color, particularly on small flowers and groups of small leaves, is by side-loading the brush and using only one or two strokes.

1. With the palette knife, mix a very small amount of varnish with some of the paint on the palette.

2. Dip the brush (it must be a square-tipped) into clear varnish, dress it slightly, and drag it across the palette, letting one side pick up some of the paint.

3. Dress the brush on the palette in one direction only until it produces a shaded stroke on the paper palette.

4. Lay the side of the brush with the most paint on the stencil at the area which shows the deepest shade. Paint a stroke to cover the desired area. A shaded color can be produced with only one stroke if the brush has been properly loaded. If it is not satisfactory, blend the color as explained under "Floating Color," page 19.

FOLIAGE

In many pictorial stencils, foliage is suggested by painting in color. The effect is achieved by blending down-curved green strokes and adding yellow highlights:

1. Mix the desired shade of green, and with a square-tipped quill paint some curved strokes (Plate 6).

2. Clean the brush as for floating color, or use a No. 8 bright's sable brush. Dip it in varnish, dress, and pull down the green paint from the bottom of the strokes in straight strokes.

3. Clean the bright's brush, pick up a small amount of varnish, and some yellow paint (chrome yellow, medium), and drag the brush across the palette until the mixture is quite dry.

4. Touch the tip of the brush to the edge of the green stroke and follow the curve of the stroke with light taps.

[34

STENCILING AND PAINTING ON VELVET

IN THE first half of the nineteenth century stenciling and painting on velvet, or theorem painting as it was called, became popular, and the interest lasted for about twenty-five years. This artistic activity was the special province of young ladies whose education was generally slanted toward their cultural development. Some of the paintings were done freehand and others were produced with stencils or theorems. It is thought that the word "theorem" may have referred to the theorem, or problem, of arranging the single stencil units into a pleasing composition; such problems were often given to young students.

Fruit, flowers, and landscapes were popular subjects. The velvet was usually white but over the years the backgrounds have mellowed to ivory or darker umber tones. Some of the more fugitive or impermanent colors have faded or almost disappeared, but the general effect of the best examples is probably more pleasing now than when they were first painted. The relatively short-lived interest in this handicraft seems surprising until one reads this early quote on the decline of velvet painting: "Frightful specimens multiplied until it has dropped into oblivion and is scarcely mentioned except in the country, where painting has not made great progress." *

About ten or fifteen years ago this type of stenciling was revived and has become extremely popular among students of Early American decoration. It offers a welcome relief from the tedious preparation and finishing processes necessary for the decoration of tin or wood. Preparing the stencil is an exacting task but the actual stenciling is, surprisingly, much easier to master than stenciling with bronze powders. Squiggles, scrolls, and fine stems, which often present a problem when painted on hard surfaces, almost seem to paint themselves on velvet.

This technique offers the decorator an opportunity to be somewhat creative since the supply of original velvets and patterns is limited and there is no concern about putting the proper design on the proper article. Good framing is important. If old frames are not available, new ones in gold or wood with gold liners are appropriate. Prints of fruit, flowers, birds, and butterflies can be broken down into stencil units and used very effectively on velvet. Evening bags, eyeglass cases, and greeting cards have been treated in this manner. Although I have never seen a stenciled velvet blouse or dress, some imaginative and ambitious decorator may already be producing one.

ENLARGING A DESIGN

If you are working from a print or design which is too small for your requirements, use the following steps to make an enlargement:

1. Determine the size of the enlargement. If you are copying a print that is

---

* Nina Fletcher Little, *The Abby Aldrich Rockefeller Folk Art Collection* (Boston; Toronto: Little, Brown and Company, 1957), p. 226. Mrs. Little quotes from *The Young Ladies' Assistant in Drawing and Painting* (Cincinnati, 1833).

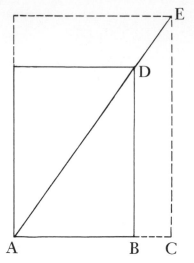

FIGURE 13 *Enlarging a design.*

4 inches high by 5 inches wide, and you want your copy to be 10 inches wide, it is simple to figure out the other dimensions—the width is twice the original, and the height would be twice the original; therefore the enlargment would be 8 by 10 inches. However, if, for example, you want the width of the enlargement to be 6¼ inches, it is not so easy to calculate the proportional width. It can be done mathematically, or by using a simple diagram (Figure 13). Extend the length of the small rectangle A–B to the desired dimension C. Draw a diagonal from A to D and extend it. Draw a perpendicular from C which will meet the diagonal at E. This line, C–E, gives you the correct width for the enlargement.

2. After deciding on the size of the enlargement, draw two rectangles on a piece of tracing paper: one of the rectangles should be the size of the original, and one the size of the enlargement. Divide all four sides of each rectangle into halves, fourths, or eighths, depending on the amount of detail in the design. The simpler the design, the fewer the divisions necessary. Draw connecting vertical and horizontal lines in pencil so that the two rectangles are broken down into proportionate small divisions —four, sixteen, or sixty-four. Numbering the lines on two sides will make it easier to follow.

3. Lay the smaller diagram over the design or print and make a careful tracing in ink.

4. Now draw the outlines freehand on the larger diagram, giving each line the same direction and placement in the larger divisions as the tracing lines have in the smaller divisions.

PREPARING THE STENCIL

The only similarity between stenciling on velvet and stenciling with bronze powders is in the use of cut-out stencils to apply the medium. When bronze powders are applied to a black background, the powder acts as the light area and the more powder that is rubbed on, the brighter the highlight; the shadow areas receive little or no powder. The reverse is true when working on white velvet. A heavy application

[36

Sandwich-edge papier-mâché tray with deco-
ration in stenciling and freehand bronze.

Owned by HSEAD, Inc. [*From* The Deco-
rator]

Reproduction of oblong tray with gold-leaf
and freehand-bronze decoration. Painted by

Walter Wright. [*From* The Ornamented
Tray]

37]

of paint produces a deep shadow and the highlight areas are stenciled with a lighter color or less paint. For this reason, and also because there is less repetition of units in the velvet designs, every single outlined section on the tracing—petal, leaf, stem, grape, etc.—must be cut out on a stencil in its proper place relative to the complete design. Even the smallest design will require several stencils since there should be at least a ½-inch space between the cut-out sections; otherwise the paint in one area could easily rub over onto another opening.

In order to determine which sections of the design should be used on each stencil, all the sections must be numbered in groups. Sometimes quicker identification is easier if colored dots are used in place of numbers.

1. Using the numeral 1 or a colored dot, mark on the tracing as many outlined sections as possible which are not adjoining. With the numeral 2 or a different color dot, mark another group of sections. These must not be close to each other but they can border on any of the first group. Continue marking until every section of the tracing has a number of colored dots and no two with similar marks are adjoining. Sometimes the final group will contain only two or three sections which cannot be put into any other group.

2. Cut as many pieces of architects' linen or stencil paper as there are numbers or colors on the tracing. These pieces must be cut the size of the velvet which is to be stenciled. Because spots of paint cannot be removed entirely, the velvet must be completely covered while it is being worked on.

3. Lay one piece of linen, dull side up, over the tracing. The tracing should be the same size as the linen so that the edges will meet exactly. Tape them together. Trace in ink all the sections marked 1 or the first color. Work carefully and try to make an exact copy of the tracing. Since each section of the design is traced twice and then cut out, there is room for some variation in the lines; but if there is too much variation the stencils will not fit together as they should.

4. Remove the linen and lay the second piece of linen in place over the tracing; tape, and then trace the second group of sections. Continue in the same way until the entire tracing has been transferred in portions to linen. Mark each piece of linen in the corner with the number or color of the sections traced.

5. Cut out all the traced units with knife and/or scissors. See page 27, "Cutting the Stencil."

PREPARING THE VELVET

The stenciling should be done on white cotton velvet. Other types of velvet have too high a pile or are too loosely woven. An ivory or pale beige color can be used, but tinting white velvet with tea seems to create the best illusion of age. Green tea produces a cool tone and orange pekoe a warmer tone.

1. Add 2 or 3 cups of boiling water to 3 tea bags, or 4 teaspoons of loose tea, and let it steep for a few minutes. (Use larger amounts for large-size velvets.) Strain the tea through a piece of cotton cloth.

[38

*Battle scene in freehand bronze with gold-leaf
and painted border. Owned by Mrs. Elizabeth
Goodwin. [From* The Decorator]

2. Cut a piece of white velvet slightly larger than the desired size and dip it
into boiling water or let it soak in warm water long enough for it to lose its opacity.
It must be completely wet.

3. Dip a test piece of wet velvet into the tea solution to check the color. It will
be slightly lighter when dry. If it is too dark, add some tap water to the solution.

4. Dip the velvet into the tested solution and lift it out. If it seems streaked or
spotty, immerse at once in hot water and start again. Do not squeeze it unless you
want a mottled effect.

5. When the color seems right, press the dripping velvet onto a window pane
with its back to the glass. If it is too drippy, it can be pressed very gently between
turkish towels before it is applied to the glass. Smooth it carefully so that it will
adhere to the glass and retain its shape while drying. If you find a few streaky areas
when the velvet is dry, don't worry; this is not undesirable as it will look more
antique.

6. Trim the edges of the velvet so that it is the right size for the frame. Roll a
piece of masking tape, sticky side out, and pick off any particles of lint from the
back of the velvet.

7. Cut a piece of contact paper the same size as the velvet and pull away about an
inch of the protective wax sheet. Press the top edge of the velvet onto the paper, pull
the wax sheet off a little farther, and smooth the velvet down onto the sticky paper,
working from the middle out to each side. Continue pulling the wax sheet with the

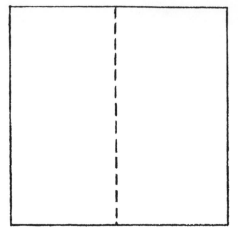

1. Score cardboard on dotted line.

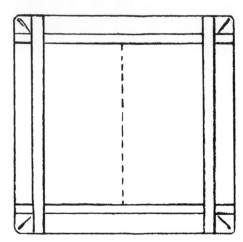

2. Tape edges of velvet on back with masking tape.

silver or aluminum

rich gold

deep gold

fire

3. Sprinkle lining powders on front of velvet.

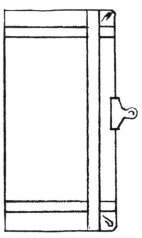

4. Fold palette, and clip.

FIGURE 14 *Making a palette for bronze powders.*

right hand, and smoothing and pressing the velvet with the left hand, until the entire piece of velvet is pressed to the contact. Smooth out any wrinkles. If contact paper is not available, mount the velvet on stiff cardboard, such as was used for the bronze-powder palette (Figure 14).

APPLYING THE STENCIL

Oil paints, principally the transparent and semitransparent colors, are used for stenciling on velvet. The three transparent colors, plus the two umbers and burnt sienna listed on the color chart (Plate 2.) with perhaps the addition of lampblack, will provide an adequate palette. However, if you find that you enjoy this technique and want to experiment, it might be interesting to try other paints or other colors. There are a number of additional transparent colors, such as scarlet and crimson lake, brown pink, Italian pink, and alizarin green. Unfortunately, some of these colors are impermanent, so if you want your velvet to be a future heirloom it would be well to avoid them. Alizarin golden (made by Grumbacher) is a warmer red than alizarin crimson, and rose doré is a beautiful shell pink. Vandyke brown might make a more pleasing brown than raw umber, and some of the less transparent colors such as cobalt blue or cerulean blue can be used. Don't mix any of the colors with white, or a completely different, and less pleasing, effect will result.

The paint can be applied with either squares of lightweight wool or brushes. The pieces of wool are wrapped around the finger as was the velvet or chamois when stenciling with powders. Bristle stencil brushes and bright's sable and bristle brushes, whichever are preferred, are useful. A separate piece of wool or a different brush should be kept for each color.

1. Squeeze small dabs of the oil colors on a paper palette and prepare the necessary color mixtures.

2. Tape the first stencil over the mounted velvet or use paper spring clips at the edges.

3. Using either the wool-covered finger or a brush, pick up a bit of paint and rub or brush it on the palette until the color shows an even tone.

4. Hold the stencil firmly in place with one hand while applying the paint with the other. Rub with a rotary motion. Use very little pressure at first until you check to see how much color appears on the velvet. If necessary, increase the pressure to get the proper value. Stencil all the sections of the same color on the first stencil; do the same with each of the other colors in turn.

The architects' linen has a tendency to slip on velvet, so make sure that when one section has been colored the stencil remains in the same position when the next section is being colored. If there is too much slippage, the next stencil will fit imperfectly and will have to be moved around to bring the sections into their proper relationship. (See *Stencil Paper* under "Supplies and Equipment.")

5. Remove stencil 1 and replace it with stencil 2. If the stencils and the velvet are the same size and the cutting and tracing have been carefully done, matching the edges of the stencils and the velvet should produce the proper register so that the sections of the design will align correctly. However, if there are some discrepancies,

Black metal cheese boat with freehand-bronze work and color washes on gold-leaf panels. [*From* The Ornamented Tray]

don't be alarmed. You will simply have to move the stencil now and then so that the proper edges will meet. Apply the color to this stencil and continue until all the stencils have been used.

6. Veins, curlycues, and fine stems must now be painted with a brush. Use a No. 2 Finepoint or similar watercolor brush for the shorter lines and curlycues, and a No. 1 or No. 2 scroller or long-pointed quill for the long, fine lines and scrolls. Dip the brush in turpentine, stroke it once or twice on the palette to remove any excess, and pick up some of the paint or paint mixture. Roll the tip of the brush on the palette to distribute the paint mixture and to produce a fine point on the brush. If a large number of lines need painting, a little turpentine can be added to the paint and the brush dipped into this. Hold the brush perpendicular and try some practice strokes on another piece of velvet. If the lines are too wide and pale, too much turpentine is being used. If the brush does not move easily on the velvet, there is probably not enough turpentine.

7. Clean the stencils very carefully on *both sides* with Energine or cleaning fluid. If there is any paint left on the underside it will come off on the next velvet on which it is used, and this will present one of the few problems in decorating which cannot be easily remedied.

8. The velvet is now ready for framing. Lay it on the glass in the frame, painted side down; back it up with heavy cardboard; and tack it in place.

WALL STENCILING

UNTIL THE TIME Janet Waring published her book *Early American Stencils on Walls and Furniture,** little was known about this form of stenciled decoration. Her research in New England, Ohio, and New York unearthed many examples of this craft and since then many more have been discovered under layers of old wallpaper. Stenciled walls are found most often in rural nineteenth-century homes for which the owners could not afford the expensive imported wallpapers. For a small fee and board and lodging, an itinerant artist might brighten the walls of several rooms with friezes, borders, or floral and fruit designs. Although undoubtedly influenced by the wallpaper patterns, the stenciler made no attempt to produce exact copies of these and the stenciled walls have a charm and dignity all their own.

Background colors were generally white, buff, or pink, although occasionally a pale blue or yellow wall has been discovered. The stencil colors were always solid with red, green, and black predominating.

Miss Waring was able to establish the identity of a number of the stencilers and to learn something of their history from descendants or, in some cases, from members of their families. Moses Eaton, Jr. was one of the most prolific of this group and was responsible for much of the decorating done in the area of Dublin,

* (Watkins Glen, N. Y.: Century House, 1937).

[42

Stenciled scenic tray with painted foliage. Owned by Helene Britt. [*From* The Ornamented Tray]

New Hampshire, where he lived for many years. The stencils found in his kit were apparently used or copied by other stencilers, so it is evident that stencil patterns were often exchanged, much as ours are today.

It would be wise when doing your first room to start with a small one. All homes do not lend themselves to this type of decoration, but a kitchen or even a bathroom will provide an excellent space for practice.

1. First plan the placement of the stencil units. If the room is small with a low ceiling and you are using only border designs, measure the length of each border unit and the length of each area to be stenciled and calculate the number of repeats. If there is a fraction left over, the units can be spaced either closer together or farther apart, depending on the type of design. If it is necessary to enlarge or reduce the design to fit your needs, follow the directions for enlarging a design under "Stenciling and Painting on Velvet," page 35). When doing a more complicated design on a larger area, make a scale drawing of the walls. A good scale to use is about ½ inch for 1 foot. Include doors and windows, and figure the number and position of each stencil unit. This careful preliminary planning will save indecision and errors when you begin to stencil.

2. Prepare the walls. To be most effective the stenciling should be done on plaster which can be painted the desired color. The plaster does not need to be absolutely smooth; in fact, it should have a little "tooth," but the paint must be flat. Williamsburg Paints has a special paint formulated for wall stenciling. White is

43]

most often used for a background paint, but if you wish to tint it, experiment with very small additions of yellow ochre, raw sienna, burnt sienna, or Signcraft red (in japan) to produce the pale buff and pink occasionally found on old walls.

3. Stencils can be cut on either architects' linen, stencil paper, or wrapping paper which has been given a coat of white shellac. If you are using linen, lay the linen over the design and trace it in ink. If the heavier paper is being used, first trace the design onto tracing paper, then onto the stencil paper with graphite paper (see Chapter IX) under the tracing. Architects' linen is best to use if there is much fine cutting in the design. Follow the directions given for cutting a stencil under "Stenciling with Bronze Powders," Chapter III.

4. There are several methods of applying the paint. Decide on the method you prefer. The old stencilers apparently used stencil brushes. Some decorators use the index finger wrapped with lightweight wool, flannel, or even suede cloth, if it is not too heavy. A finger cut from a rubber glove and worn under the wool will keep your finger clean. I have found that using a stenciling pad makes the process quicker and less tiring. A stenciling pad is like a large bob and it can be made in several sizes. Pull off a fair-sized amount of absorbent cotton and fold the edges over toward the center, leaving a smooth surface on the bottom. Lay it on a square of flannel, pull the edges of the flannel together tightly, and wind it with thread or secure it with a rubber band. A large stenciling pad might be about the size of a golf ball. A separate pad can be made for each color or a single one can be reused by wrapping a piece of plastic, and then another piece of flannel, around the original pad. The second piece of flannel can then be removed and replaced for use with another color.

5. On a paper palette or folded newspaper, mix the paint for each color in the design. Mix enough paint to finish the entire room because matching the colors when remixing could be frustrating and time-consuming. Use japan paints. These are available in a variety of colors but small amounts of oil color can be added to get the proper mixture. Use plenty of white because the colors will appear darker when applied on the light wall. At the end of each work period either cover the remaining paint in Saran Wrap, or immerse in water so that the paint will remain soft.

6. Tape the stencil in the proper place on the wall with masking tape. Start with the frieze stencil and do this all the way around the room before going on to the others.

7. Pour a little turpentine into a jar cover. Moisten the brush or cloth in the turpentine and then dip it into the paint. Rub it on newspaper to distribute the paint evenly. With the fingers of the free hand, hold the stencil firmly against the wall near the area being colored. When using a brush, each opening must be worked on until it is completely colored. The finger or pad can be rubbed back and forth over a series of openings of the same color. If the paint is too thick it will take longer to cover the background. If the correct proportion of paint and turpentine is used, the paint should rub on easily and leave clean, sharp edges.

8. Clean the back of the stencil with cleaning fluid if paint has leaked through onto the back. If the edges of the stencil become curled or bent, it may be necessary

Stenciled tray, Mary and Her Little Lamb.
[*From* The Ornamented Tray]

Oblong tray with stenciled double border.
[*From* The Ornamented Tray]

to cut another stencil to finish the job. Since japan paints dry very quickly, it is not always necessary to clean the stencil thoroughly before putting it away unless the paint has built up to such an extent that the openings have changed shape. The stencil brush should be cleaned in turpentine and then washed with soap and water. Moisten the pad in turpentine and rub it on newspaper to get off most of the paint before storing. If there are any unwanted spots of paint on the wall, let them dry and paint over them with the background color.

Oblong handhole tray with repeat stenciled border on floor and gold-leaf border on flange, with stormont work between units. [*From* The Ornamented Tray]

IV

Freehand Bronze

FREEHAND BRONZE is a term used to describe any part of a design which is first painted and then rubbed or dusted with bronze powder. The method is very similar to stenciling; however, instead of applying the bronze powder through stencils with cut-out forms, the design units are painted with black or colored enamel paint or black seal. When this paint becomes tacky, the powder is applied with velvet or with a brush, and it can be solid or shaded, just as in stenciling.

The freehand-bronze form of decoration is found on some of the earliest of decorated pieces. It was used in combination with painting, gold and silver leaf, and later with stenciling. Many of these early pieces, which were produced in Pontypool, Wales, and other English and Welsh towns, were copies or adaptations of the beautiful lacquer work imported from the Orient in the seventeenth century. These imitations by both Dutch and English craftsmen were referred to as "japanned ware," and the methods they used were adapted to allow for differences in climate and the availability of materials.

Designs that include freehand bronzing are especially popular with students of decoration, perhaps because of the limited supply as well as the beautiful effects achieved by this method of handling the bronze powders. Combinations of fruit, flowers, and leaves used as center designs on light-colored or bronzed backgrounds, or on gold or white bands, are typical designs. Large black trays showing entire battle scenes or other scenes with groups of people and animals are rare finds, but few decorators have the courage or patience to reproduce these elaborate designs.

47]

SUPPLIES AND EQUIPMENT

Black Enamel and Seal   There are a number of good brands of enamel paint, such as Lowe Brothers' Plax, Du Pont's Duco, or that of Sherwin-Williams. Seal or black varnish dries more slowly than the enamel. For this reason it should be used for designs that require more time to be produced. Craftint and Gile's black seal are good. The latter, which seems to be especially popular, can be bought at some art stores or from Gile's Varnish Company, College Point, New York.

Making a Bob   Cut a piece of velvet about 1 inch square and place a small wad of absorbent cotton in the center. Pull the velvet tightly around the cotton and wind thread around the ends, leaving a ball of velvet. Winding masking tape around the velvet ends will form a short handle. The size of the bob depends on the amount of cotton. It is a good idea to make several sizes.

Charcoal Stumps   Used for blending charcoal drawings, these stumps are small paper cylinders pointed at one or both ends. They can be bought in several sizes at art supply stores.

Bright's Brush   See Chapter I, "Supplies and Equipment."

EXECUTING THE DESIGN

IT WOULD BE wise to practice painting some simple units from a freehand-bronze design before attempting to paint a complete pattern or tray. Solid gold areas should be painted first; and their quality depends almost entirely on the painting underneath. When a design contains a combination of treatments and techniques, a rule which should be remembered when reproducing such a design is: Paint *first*, all solid gold areas (gold leaf or bronze powder); *secondly*, all shaded gold or silver areas; and *lastly*, all painted units which have no application of bronze powder. The reason for this order will be obvious if you ever do it in reverse. Even though they seem to be dry, the painted areas which should have no solid or shaded gold can easily pick up some of the powder or gold leaf when the areas designed for the bronze powder or gold leaf are being covered. A very slight tackiness, which is enough to cause leaf or powder to adhere, can remain in the paint for some time.

SOLID UNITS

IN FREEHAND BRONZING, solid units are those parts of the design which are completely covered with the bronze powder. Unlike the shaded units which must be painted in a color to contrast with the powders (see next section), the solid units can be painted in whatever color will show most clearly on the background paint. Black varnish called seal, or black enamel should be used on light-colored backgrounds, and red or yellow enamel (Lowe Brothers' Plax is excellent) on black

[48

backgrounds. This contrast will make it possible to check on the quality of your strokes. Be sure that the edges are clean; the points sharp; and the paint smooth, not ridgy.

1. Trace the design, mount the tracing, and cover with acetate as described in Chapter II.

2. Pour some seal or enamel paint into a metal bottle cap and place it on the palette. Load the proper brush as you did for country painting, and paint the design.

3. When the paint is tacky—about the same tack used for stenciling—rub on the bronze powder with the velvet-covered finger. Polish well.

4. After the design has dried for twenty-four to forty-eight hours, wash off the excess powder with water or mild soap and water (Dreft seems to work quite well for this operation). If a cloudiness still remains around the units, try erasing it with a kneaded rubber eraser. This cloudiness will be more obvious on a black background such as a tray, or on the acetate, when it is mounted on black paper or cardboard.

When painting solid units on patterns, coarse powders can be substituted for lining powders. They are more brilliant and the excess can be removed more easily.

SHADED UNITS

THE BASE COATS for shaded freehand-bronze units are generally painted black with enamel paint or black seal. Green leaves, especially those found in Chippendale-like flowers, are often treated with bronze powders, and occasionally red or blue units appear in a freehand-bronze design. These colored base coats can be painted with a mixture of tube colors and varnish. It helps to use japan colors for these mixtures, as they have better covering quality and require less drying time. Japan paints are available in a range of colors other than the red, yellow, and white mentioned in the basic list (see page 234 and Plate 2). If oil colors are used, add as much varnish as you can without thinning the paint so much that the background shows through. The oil paint takes a very long time to dry, so the tack is produced by the varnish.

When units overlap, finish the part which appears to be in the foreground and allow this to dry thoroughly before painting the area which appears to be behind the first one. In a large design where two units touch, paint only one in the first painting so that you will have more freedom when applying the powder.

1. Lay a piece of acetate over your tracing of the outline and paint the unit, using enamel paint or black seal (Figure 15 and Plate 7).

2. After waiting an hour or more, test the paint for tackiness. This can be done with a piece of linen, as described in Chapter III, or by touching the paint very lightly with the finger near the edge of the unit. If the finger pulls away with only slight adhesion, the paint is probably ready for the powder. Gile's black seal, which is especially satisfactory for this work, dries very slowly and holds its tack for a long time, so there is no need to panic if you are interrupted while waiting for the proper tack. For this reason some decorators paint entire trays with the seal when they are applying a complicated stenciled design.

FIGURE 15 *Full-size tracings for freehand-bronze units.*

3. Pick up some bronze powder on velvet or chamois wrapped around the index finger, or a brush. Start rubbing the unit in the highlight area and blend toward the edge as in stenciling. If the powder does not shade off easily, or if the velvet or brush pulls a bit, the paint is probably too wet. Bad stenciling and poor freehand-bronze work more often results from paint that is too wet, than paint that is almost dry. The shading can be done with velvet or with a brush. The process compares to stenciling except that the edge of the painted unit replaces the cut edge of the stencil. Most freehand-bronze fruit is powdered fairly close to the edge, leaving only a faint shaded black line. If two colors of bronze powder are used, be sure to start rubbing the second color in the highlight area of the first color and then blend off.

4. After twenty-four to forty-eight hours have passed, wash the design with mild soap and water, dry, apply a coat of clear varnish (see "Varnishing," Chapter X), and allow to dry for at least twenty-four hours.

5. Paint any additional strokes, overstrokes, or washes of transparent color last. The floating color can be applied as it is in stenciling except that the paint-and-varnish mixture cannot be allowed to go over the edges onto the background when it is not black. Mistakes can be wiped off, when fresh, with varnish.

Using a Bob and Stump

A bob, which must be made (see page 48), is like a miniature velvet-covered finger and is useful in spots where the finger is too large to do a good job. Some decorators prefer to fold or twist a piece of velvet so that the point of the fold acts as a tiny bob. In this case the velvet can be refolded for use with another shade of powder and no one spot becomes worn as it does with a bob.

Charcoal stumps are used to produce little strokelike highlights, often done in silver on leaves, fruit, and backgrounds. They come in several sizes—some large ones with blunt ends, and some smaller ones with sharp points. The pointed stumps are used for making fine gold or silver lines, and the tips can be rubbed on fine sandpaper to produce a blunt tip. Try making some of the short straight strokes first, using a slightly blunted stump (Plate 7).

1. Dip the tip of the stump into silver or gold bronze powder, and rotate the point in the palm of the hand. If you object to getting powder on your hand, rotate the stump on the paper palette. This distributes the powder evenly on the tip.

2. Be sure that the paint or seal has the proper tack. If it is too wet, the stump will not deposit the powder but will pick up the black. Grasp the stump like a pencil, but use the side for making the stroke.

3. Press the side of the tip onto the tacky surface and draw it toward you and then up to feather off. Although the stump work on fine originals appears to be done in single strokes, we often have to doctor our first attempts to create the proper effect. If the stroke is too sharp, work on it with a tiny brush to soften the edges. Use either a No. 1 or No. 2 short-pointed quill or a No. 0 or No. 1 bright's red sable. Some decorators start with the brush and then sharpen up the solid area with the stump. After some practice you will find the method that works best for you.

The designs on the ends of this stenciled bread tray are also found on apple trays. [From The Ornamented Tray]

Using a Brush

THE USE of a brush such as a No. 2 or No. 4 short-pointed quill for blending bronze powders has been described under "Stenciling," Chapter III. Such brushes are also useful in freehand-bronze work, especially when applying bronze powder to the edges of leaves where the powder must blend toward the center with no line showing. In designs where the application of bronze powder should look like a soft, straight brush stroke—larger than the tiny ones described above—a bright's red sable, No. 4 to No. 8, does a good job. Dip the brush in the bronze powder and tap each side on the palette. Using the "knife" edge, brush the stroke toward you and pull up to blend the "tail."

V

Gold Leaf

GOLD IN ALL its various forms is unrivaled as a decorative metal. The art of beating gold into thin sheets, or leaf, was known as early as 3000 B.C. It was a technique employed by ancient Egyptians and Orientals.

Pure gold is too soft for ordinary use in leaf form, so other metals such as silver or copper are often added. A high silver content produces a lemon or pale gold leaf, while additions of copper make deep gold shades. Pure gold resists tarnish, but when alloyed with other metals discoloration eventually develops. Twenty-three karat gold leaf, with only a small percentage of silver or copper, is the least subject to tarnishing and is therefore preferred for decorating. Silver leaf tarnishes quickly and is not recommended for use, except on glass, because even a coat of shellac or varnish will not prevent a change in color. A satisfactory substitute is palladium leaf. Palladium is a rare metallic element of the platinum group that is silver-white in color and very malleable.

The finest quality gold leaf is called glass gold, for it has the greatest uniformity of thickness and a minimum of pinholes, cracks, and repaired surfaces. Each leaf is placed between sheets of tissue which have been rubbed with jewelers' rouge. So-called patent gold leaf comes mounted on tissues ready to apply, and is used when working outdoors. It can be used in tray work, if desired, but it seems to lack some of the luster of the unmounted leaf.

Gilding is the process of applying to a surface all types of metal leaf and bronzing powders. A *size* is the vehicle by which the leaf or powder is made to adhere to the surface. Either a quick or a slow size can be used on wood or metal, but for our

FIGURE 16   *Full-size tracings for gold-leaf units.*

purposes a quick-drying size is more satisfactory. When gold or silver leaf is used on glass or burnished on picture frames, the process is quite different, and other types of size are used.

Gold leaf is found on antique tin and wood, alone or combined with all the techniques described, except country painting. When combined with painting—as on Chippendale or lace-edge trays—it is usually used for the border design. Sometimes gold leaf is etched and shaded with umbers to give it form; occasionally it is glazed with transparent color.

SUPPLIES AND EQUIPMENT

Gold Leaf   Gold leaf and palladium leaf (used as a substitute for silver) are sold in small books which contain twenty-five leaves, each about 3⅜ inches square. The best quality of gold leaf is called glass gold. It is available in three shades: deep gold or XX (23-karat), lemon gold (18-karat), and pale gold (16-karat). Gold leaf is available where decorating supplies are sold.

Imitations   So-called Dutch, German, and Italian metal, and aluminum leaf, are imitations of gold and silver. The sheets are much thicker than gold-leaf sheets and are about 5 inches square. They can be laid in the same way as gold leaf, but they cannot be etched. Their only value to the decorator might be as a substitute on patterns or on backgrounds. If you are in any doubt as to whether metal leaf is gold or an imitation, rub a bit of it between your fingers; if it is real gold, it will disintegrate and disappear. Real gold also has a greenish cast when help up to the light.

A comparatively new product that can be used to give a gold effect on solid areas is called Treasure Gold. This is a metallic wax finish, available in several shades, which can be rubbed on wood or painted surfaces. It is obtainable at art supply stores.

Etching Tools   A *single etcher* is a sharp, pointed tool. Any one of a number of different articles can be used: a dentist's pick; a very hard pencil, well sharpened; or even a stylus with the tip ground to a point. An etching tool can also be made by inserting a large needle into a holder.

A *triple etcher* can be bought or made. To make one, hold three equally sized needles—laid flat and touching each other—between pliers, and keeping the points aligned, apply solder to the eye ends. Let the solder harden; then put some solder in the slot of a pen holder, and insert the needles in the slot. To strengthen the etcher, add more solder to the needles to within about ½ inch of the points. (See diagram, Figure 17.)

Stand Oil and Mastic Varnish   Both stand oil and mastic varnish are materials used in canvas painting; they can be purchased at art supply stores.

Reproductions of box and coffin trays with country painting. Box (LOWER LEFT) painted by Helene Britt. Tray (LOWER RIGHT) *painted by Margaret Emery. [From* The Decorator]

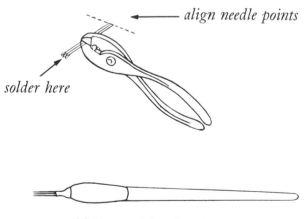

align needle points

solder here

FIGURE 17   *Making a triple etcher.*

Gilder's Cushion   This is a piece of wood, about 5 by 9 inches, padded, and tightly covered with a leather such as capeskin. It can be purchased at an art supply store, but if you don't want to invest in one for only limited use, you can cut the gold leaf in the book, if you work very carefully. Open the book from the *back* and press the center fold so that it will lie flat on the table. Hold the book down with one hand and cut the sheet with the sharp knife. Make sure that there are no sheets of leaf behind the one you are cutting. The cover and rouge paper act as a slight cushion.

Gilder's Tip   A flat brush about 4 inches wide made of badger or squirrel hair, with a section of cardboard in place of a handle, is called a gilder's tip. Available at art supply stores.

PICKING THE PROPER SIZE

IF THE gold leaf is to be etched, and the etching lines are to be black, a black enamel or seal must be used. On rare occasions, the etching is found to be the color of the colored background; in these cases a clear varnish, gold size, or an enamel paint the color of the ground can be used.

If the gold leaf is not etched, use red, yellow, or black enamel, varnish, or gold size.

For very fine lines, which might dry too quickly with an enamel paint, use either of the following mixtures:
  (a) one-half yellow enamel
       one-quarter mastic varnish
       one-quarter stand oil and turpentine, mixed (devised by Walter Wright)

  (b) yellow enamel with a few drops of slow gold size.
  If the article is to be kept outdoors, use Heinz or LeFranc's slow oil size.

PAINTING THE DESIGN

WHEN PAINTING a pattern or practicing, use either black cardboard or acetate. Black cardboard is more satisfactory when there is etching to be done since it is firmer than the acetate. If cardboard is used, the pattern must be traced on the cardboard. (See directions in Chapter IX for transferring a pattern.) If the pattern is to be painted on acetate, set up as for country painting. Bronze powder is often substituted for gold leaf on patterns to save expense.

   1. If you are painting a design, give the article a coat of varnish, let dry for several days, and then rub with No. 0000 steel wool. If the varnished surface is quite bumpy, use wet-or-dry sandpaper No. 600 (see "Finishing," Chapter X) dipped in water. *The surface must be very smooth.*

   2. Shake a little talcum powder onto the design area and brush with a soft brush, leaving only a *thin* film.

3. Trace the design, using lithopone powder or graphite paper, depending on the color of the background (see Chapter IX).

4. Pour some of the proper size into a bottle cap.

5. Powder your fingers to prevent accidentally touching the background and creating a spot to which the gold leaf might adhere.

6. Select the proper brush for the required strokes, load it, and dress it well so that the strokes will have clean edges and sharp points. Paint the design, doing the large areas first since they take longer to set up, or get tacky.

7. Test the tack carefully with the fingertip. The best time to lay gold leaf is when the size is almost dry but still tacky enough to hold the leaf, probably a little drier than for stenciling. The leaf will have much more luster if applied at this time. It will appear dull if laid when the painted design is too wet.

APPLYING THE LEAF

1. Lift the cover of a book of glass gold leaf very slowly, being careful not to breathe directly on the leaf. Slip a 4 inch square of wax paper over the sheet of leaf and close the book.

2. Rub the cover firmly with the finger and carefully open the book again. Lift out the wax paper to which the leaf has adhered and close the book. Be careful not to touch the leaf, and when laying it on the table, be sure that the leaf side is up. If using patent gold leaf, which is already mounted on tissues, simply remove a sheet from the book.

3. If the area to be covered is small, the mounted leaf can be cut into convenient sizes with sharp shears.

4. Lay the mounted leaf, leaf side down, on the smaller units of the design first and rub firmly with the fingers, holding the paper in place with the other hand. Use a little extra pressure on the edges of the painted units as they usually dry faster.

5. Lift off the wax paper or tissue and if enough leaf remains on the paper press it onto another part of the design. It is not necessary to use a piece which will cover the entire unit. When the loose gold is brushed off, no lines are evident where several small pieces have been used to cover a large area. Don't try to save pieces of wax paper on which there are remnants of leaf for more than a few days, for eventually the leaf adheres permanently to the wax paper.

6. If the gold leaf is laid *when the size has reached the right tack*, the loose gold can be brushed off almost immediately. Using a soft, flat, camel- or squirrel-hair brush held at a 25-degree angle or absorbent cotton, remove all the loose gold. Work *very carefully*. If the leaf seems to be scratched, let it dry longer.

7. If there are any holidays (spots where the gold has not adhered), press some gold leaf on that area; there should be enough tack in the size to receive it. If it does not stick, try breathing on the spot and then laying the gold leaf. All repairs of this sort should be made before the size is completely dry since it is impossible to patch later on without spoiling the appearance of the gold leaf.

[58

8. Several hours later the leaf can be given a slight burnishing by wiping it with a piece of absorbent cotton moistened with very hot water and then wiping it dry with cotton.

STENCILING WITH GOLD LEAF

SINCE TIME was of the essence when stenciled trays were being produced by the thousands, gold leaf was laid through a stencil onto the tacky surface prepared to receive the bronze powders. This method of laying gold leaf was used only when one unit was to be done in gold leaf. When making a copy of a tray of

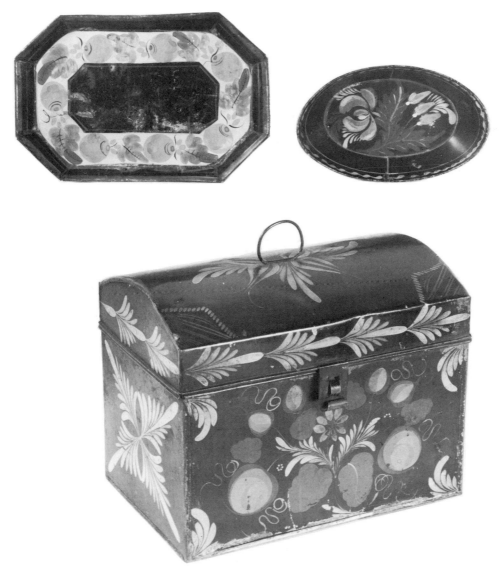

ABOVE: *Coffin and oblong trays with country painting.* BELOW: *Tin trunk, or document box, with country painting. Owned by HSEAD, Inc.* [*From* The Ornamented Tray]

this kind it is not necessary to lay the gold leaf by this method, but it might be interesting to know how it was probably done on the original.

1. Lay the stencil that is cut out in the shape of the gold-leaf unit on the tacky varnish and press down the edges.

2. Place several extra pieces of architects' linen around the edge of the stencil to assure a large area of linen between the stencil and the remainder of the background.

3. Remove a sheet of gold leaf which has been mounted on wax paper from the book and lay it, leaf side down, over the stencil.

4. Rub firmly with the finger and press around the edges of the stencil.

5. Lift the wax paper very carefully so that no loose gold drifts onto the background. If the edges of the unit look ragged, pick up some gold (from the wax paper) on the tip of a bright's sable brush and push it against the edges of the stencil. Be sure that the edges of the stencil have not lifted from the background at any point.

6. When the unit seems to be well covered with leaf, very carefully and lightly pick up all particles of loose gold on a piece of absorbent cotton and gently lift off the stencil. Corrections or etching can be done when the varnished background is thoroughly dry.

MAKING REPAIRS ON GOLD LEAF

IT WAS mentioned earlier that repairs in the laying of the gold leaf should be done before the size is completely dry. Other repairs can wait until later. If edges are rough, the excess gold can be scraped off very carefully with an X-acto knife. To assure a good job, cut a piece of cardboard or heavy paper to conform to the edge to be repaired and lay it over the rough area. With a very sharp No. 8H pencil or single etcher, score the gold leaf, using the cardboard as a guide. Remove the cardboard and scrape off the excess gold up to the scored line. If much repairing is necessary it is better to wipe off the section and repaint. To wipe off, first use turpentine, then Energine, and when the section is completely gone, allow the surface to dry and *apply more talcum powder* before repainting.

ETCHING (PLATE 8)

GOLD-LEAF designs are sometimes etched to create shadow areas in the various units, thus giving them a feeling of form. The etching on old designs is usually quite simple but some beginners, especially those with an art background, have a tendency to overetch in an effort to produce realism. (See tracing patterns in Figure 16.)

1. Do the etching within twenty-four hours. If it is done before the underpainting is dry, the lines will be wider. If left too long, it will be difficult to cut through to the underpainting with the etching needle.

2. If the etching is too complicated to do freehand, lay the tracing of the design

over the gold leaf, and with a stylus, trace just a *few* lines—only enough to define the general areas of etching. It is not necessary to use a transfer paper.

3. Use a single etcher for single lines and a triple etcher for areas of shading. When using the triple etcher, always start the stroke at the point where the shading should be the heaviest. The etching usually follows the curve of the object being shaded.

If the gold leaf has been left too long to be etched, the lines can be added with a crow-quill pen and drawing ink, although it is more difficult to get the desired effect. This should be done after the gold leaf has been varnished and rubbed with steel wool No. 0000.

Shading with Paint

1. Give the decoration a coat of gloss varnish and allow to dry thoroughly. Rub with No. 0000 steel wool and clean off.

2. For *dry-brush shading*, use a sable bright's or an old sable brush which has been cut off about ⅛ to ¼ inch above the ferrule. Squeeze a little burnt umber onto the palette. Dip the brush into the paint and rub on the palette until an even tone appears. Start rubbing on the gold leaf area where the etching is the heaviest and taper off as it gets lighter (Plate 8).

3. When the umber shading seems to be done with strokes, paint as you would for country tin, using enough varnish with the paint to make the strokes somewhat transparent.

4. If transparent color is floated over the gold leaf, follow the directions on pages 19–20 for floating color.

Stormont, Fine Lines, and Squiggles

In his book, *Pontypool and Usk Japanned Ware*,* W. D. John writes: "From 1790 until the close of japannery the stormont (a term possibly derived from the name of a contemporary statesman whose speeches were apt to wander considerably) or continuous meandering line patterns of different widths were most popular, the whole surface being covered, often over a crimson ground color."

This wiggly, meandering line is usually gold leaf and must be done freehand, since it would be impossible to follow a tracing line. Stormont work was used in border designs to fill the gaps between units and to create a lacy effect (Plate 8).

1. Prepare the area to be decorated as it was done for gold leaf. Dust a thin layer of talcum powder over the area.

2. Mix a drop or two of turpentine with some yellow enamel in a bottle cap.

3. A crow-quill pen can be used for very fine lines and a coarser penpoint (Estabrook No. 128 is recommended) for heavier lines. Dip the penpoint into the enamel. Don't dip it in very far—just barely touch it.

* (Newport, England: Ceramic Book Company, 1953).

4. Practice making lines on black cardboard first. You may have a little difficulty getting the paint to start flowing. If it doesn't flow at all, thin the mixture just a bit more with turpentine. If there is too much turpentine the line will spread.

5. Check the tack periodically. You will probably be able to cover 3 or 4 inches with stormont before it is ready for the gold leaf. Clean the pen and reload frequently.

6. Apply the gold leaf on the lines and brush off the loose gold as previously described.

Fine lines and squiggles in gold leaf can be handled the same way. However, the groups of fine lines which are often found dripping from Chippendale borders are more effectively done with a brush. Use the mixture listed under "Picking the Proper Size" (page 57) and a No. 1 scroller.

APPLYING GOLD LEAF TO IRREGULAR SURFACES

WHEN APPLYING gold leaf to objects with irregular or ornate surfaces such as frames, weathervanes, sculpture, etc., it is not practical to use the mounted sheet since it would touch only the raised portions of the surface. Antique mirror and picture frames were generally gilded partly with burnished gold leaf. This is a highly specialized process not within the province of this book and it should not be confused with the slight polishing (referred to as burnishing) done with a brush or absorbent cotton. So-called matte gold, which is the result of the following process, was used with the burnished gold as a contrast to the high luster, but can be quite effective in itself.

1. Paint the entire surface (which should be perfectly clean) with varnish or quick gold size. Weathervanes or anything to be used outdoors should be painted with slow oil size.

2. If the gold is to be applied in small pieces, open a book of gold leaf very carefully, turn it over, and press the sheet onto a gilder's cushion ("Supplies and Equipment," page 57). With a sharp, straight-edged knife, cut the leaf into convenient sizes. If the gold leaf sticks to the knife, rub the cutting edge with a piece of rouge paper from the book. If the article is large and the gold leaf will be applied in whole sheets, they can be removed directly from the book.

3. When the size has reached the proper tack, pick up a gilder's tip ("Supplies and Equipment," page 57) and brush it across your cheek once or twice (if your skin is very dry, you could rub it with a little cold cream). Next lay the straight tip of the brush just over the edge of the piece of leaf, pull the sheet out of the book or off the cushion, and hold it with the leaf hanging down from the brush. It can then be flipped onto the tacky surface. This whole operation should be done rather quickly and with authority, which will need some practice. If there is any hesitation when picking up the gold leaf, it sometimes leaps towards the brush and becomes crumpled before the brush has been laid on the proper spot.

4. Use the flat camel-hair brush you used for removing excess gold (but use the tip this time instead of the side). Push the gold leaf into all the indentations so that the

area is entirely covered. On small pieces, a bright's sable brush size No. 8 or No. 10 is helpful. You will probably have to lay several sheets of leaf on the same area before it is completely covered.

5. When the object is completely covered, brush it thoroughly with the soft camel-hair brush to remove all the loose gold. This also gives a slight burnish to the high spots. Articles gilded in this manner are not generally varnished, as this spoils the rich appearance of the gold. However, if you want to create an antique effect, give the article a coat of varnish and antique it with umber, as described in Chapter X.

Bread tray with country painting, Grand-mother's Rose. *Owned by HSEAD, Inc.*
[*From* The Ornamented Tray]

VI

Chippendale Painting

T HE CHIPPENDALE type of decorative painting was used principally on metal or papier-mâché trays with scalloped edges. These were referred to as Chippendale, Pie Crust, or Gothic trays, and the trays with broad flattened edges were called Sandwich Gothic. They first appeared in England and Wales about 1760 and were produced for over a century. Later the same type of painting was often used on rectangular, oval, Queen Anne, and Victorian trays.

The early examples of Chippendale painting had rather subdued gold-leaf patterns with flowers only on the borders. In the early 1800s artists created designs for the floors of the trays, showing exquisite handling of flowers, birds, and fountains. The decoration became increasingly more elaborate and eventually included just about everything in the decorator's repertory. The border designs were usually delicate scrolls in either gold leaf or a rusty red with fine gold-leaf lines and lots of "drippy moss." Oriental scenes were also popular. Backgrounds were generally black, sometimes bronzed, but occasionally one finds a Gothic tray painted a dark red, blue, or white. When first introduced to this type of decoration, beginners, and especially those with contemporary tastes, often find it too busy and quite unattractive. However, after studying all the techniques involved, they sometimes find the reproduction of an elaborate Chippendale design to be an interesting challenge, and by the time the painting is finished they have built up a respect bordering on reverence for the artist's skill. During the latter part of the nineteenth century the workmanship deteriorated and the later examples of Chippendale painting were coarsely executed in gaudy colors.

Country painting made very little attempt to give any form to the flowers, fruit, and leaves in the design. Usually a few lighter and darker strokes or floated color were added over the base coats to represent highlights and shadows, but for the most part design was more important than form. Chippendale painting, on the other hand, rendered the objects more realistically and although the painting was stylized, some of the flowers look as if they could be plucked from the tray, even though they do not always bear a very close resemblance to nature's original.

It is sometimes impossible to establish the botanical identity of a flower; in these cases it is referred to as a "tray flower."

The filmy, translucent effect of Chippendale painting was achieved by building up the form of the flower with layers of paint, working from transparent to the opaque colors, and then floating transparent color over the modeled flower. This so-called indirect method of painting was used by many of the Old Masters such as Van Eyck, Rubens, and Rembrandt. It gives a stronger three-dimensional effect and more luminous color than the direct method of mixing the desired colors and applying them in one step.

The ability to paint flowers with the beautiful misty quality found on the best examples of Chippendale painting is the special goal of most decorators, and it seems to be the most elusive. Directions for painting base coats and floating color can be followed to the letter but "veiling" the flower or adding the final petals requires additional practice. One has to get a feeling for the contour of the flower so that the petals will look flowing and unlabored. Students with a knowledge of drawing have some advantage in this area, as they are familiar with the use of light and shade to produce form. For the student without this training, the following information may be helpful.

SUPPLIES AND EQUIPMENT

The Spotter   This is a red-sable watercolor brush sold by Art & Sign Brush Manufacturing Corporation. It is a good brush to use for flower painting, especially the lace-edge type (Chapter VII), as it does not have an extremely fine point and the paint mixture can be concentrated in the tip. Any other good red-sable brush of this kind would be adequate.

MODELING WITH LIGHT AND SHADE

FLOWER PAINTING should be approached with the total shapes of the flowers in mind rather than with any immediate concern for the individual petals. These total shapes, as well as almost any solid object, can be reduced to four simple geometric shapes or combinations and modifications of these, much as the painting of country base coats was simplified by breaking them down into combinations of brush strokes.

The ability to recognize these shapes and treat the objects accordingly is especially helpful when working from only a tracing or when restoring a painting in which part of the design is missing. If you know how to create the illusion of form in these four shapes, you will be able to handle the shading of related objects. In both stenciling and painting, solid objects which are not given the proper shading will appear two-dimensional—that is, they will seem to have been cut out and pasted on the background.

The drawings of the cube, sphere, cone, and cylinder in Figure 18 are shown first in a line drawing, then in light and shade, and finally in an adaptation to some form found in decoration. Although the shading on these forms is treated realistically, the structure of the flower forms, which resemble the stylized treatment used by many of the Chippendale painters, are not necessarily botanically accurate. Study the structure of flowers in seed catalogues. A fine decorator should be familiar with the natural shapes before ignoring the rules to get special effects.

FIGURE 18   *Using light and shade to create form.*

1. The cube is the only one of the four forms on which all the planes or sides meet at an angle. Notice that on such an object the shading changes instantly from light to dark, leaving a sharp edge. On curved surfaces the shading changes gradually so that there is no line of demarcation between the light and dark areas. As a decorative form, the cube is found most often in scenic designs involving buildings, bridges, and architectural details. In the fourth sketch a second cube has been cut on the diagonal and a half placed on the first cube. Details added in the last sketch give the impression of a building.

2. A circle becomes a sphere when rendered in light and shade. The third figure is indented so that it resembles the general shape of the cuplike portion of a rose; in the fourth sketch petals have been indicated to add to the illusion. Notice that the outlines of the inside petals curve toward the upper dot in the center of the depression. The outside petals curve toward the lower dot. Both dots serve as imaginary attachment points for the petals and would not, of course, be a part of the painting. The outlines of the petals around the solid center portion, or "cup," must follow the horizontal curve of the sphere. Unless the strokes which represent petals on any flower follow the proper curves, no amount of fine shading will make them look right.

3. The cone is shown first in a line drawing, then in light and shade, and in the third sketch it has been tipped back and shaded to appear hollow. In the fourth sketch two cones, one narrower than the other, have been attached to represent the funnel and petals of a morning glory. In the last sketch the outline of a morning glory has been added. Notice that the vanishing point for the petal strokes is in the funnel and they are curved because the lower portion of the flower flares out.

4. The cylinder is rendered in a line drawing, and in light and shade. In the next sketch two small cylinders and the outline of a tree trunk have been added. In the fourth sketch the cylinder has been laid on its side and petals outlined on the curved surface. The last sketch shows portions of two attached cylinders with the outline of a leaf superimposed.

PAINTING CHIPPENDALE FLOWERS

BASE COATS FOR FLOWERS

When painting the flowers in a Chippendale design, first determine the color and thinness of the base coats. They were generally white, in varying degrees of transparency; but occasionally orange-red was used in place of white for red flowers. If you are working from an old tray which is to be stripped, scrape off the top layers of paint on one spot with an X-acto knife. If the tray is to be restored, experiment with different combinations of base coats and floated color until the proper effect is achieved. If you are working from a pattern which has been painted on acetate, look at the back, if possible, to check on the color of the first layer of paint.

MODELING THE FLOWERS

When modeling a flower by using transparent to opaque whites on a black background, the background acts as the shadow area and the opaque white provides the highlight. Therefore, the thinner the white paint (more varnish in the mixture), the more the background shows through to produce a deeper shadow. A very general rule for painting a simple flower is: (1) a thin white base coat; (2) when dry, heavier white petals just inside the outline of the base coat; (3) when dry, floated transparent color; (4) when dry, another layer of white petals or accents; (5) when dry, strokes and dots for the center. Sometimes the flowers are modeled completely in thin-to-opaque whites with a final wash of transparent color (see rose C, Plate 11).

LEAVES

Leaves painted in the Chippendale manner appear in many different shades of green, from light yellow-green to deep blue-green. There is less effort made to create realism in the leaves than in the flowers. The green base coats are flat and opaque, and are sometimes rubbed with bronze powder when tacky. Two or three layers of translucent or opaque overstrokes in color represent shadows and veins.

BIRDS

Birds were usually painted over metal leaf, bronze powder, or white base coats or combinations of these.

PRELIMINARY EXERCISES IN PAINTING

IF YOU will take the time to practice painting the base coats and strokes before attempting to paint a flower, you will find flower painting much easier. After attaining some degree of proficiency, you will approach the painting of the flower with much less timidity and the result will be infinitely more satisfactory.

In Figure 19(A) three base coats are shown which have been painted in three different degrees of transparency. It is not always necessary to make the value absolutely uniform, as succeeding layers of paint will cover most of it except the outer edges. Dip a square-tipped quill (No. 3 or No. 5, depending on the size of the base coat) into varnish and then into striping white in japan, and dress the brush on a piece of black paper until the desired value is attained. Paint with large strokes, letting the edge of the brush make the outline, and pull the strokes toward the center.

The strokes in Figure 19(B) are painted with a side-loaded brush. Load the brush, as described in Chapter III under "Floating Color with Side-Loaded Brush." In this case, you would use white paint instead of a transparent color, but the process is the same. After dipping the brush (a square-tipped quill) into the varnish, dress it once or twice on the palette before picking up the paint. If there is too much varnish

[68

PLATE 5   Applying the stencil. *Peach:* start with the highlight and blend as indicated. *Pear:* stencil three small highlights and blend out. *Grapes:* for a whole grape, stencil a highlight and add a line of silver around the shadow edge. For partial grapes, stencil the lower edge and blend off toward the overlapping grape. *Melon:* always shown partially behind other units, melons must be blended off before reaching the bottom of the stencil. Use two shades of powder as indicated. *Silhouette:* stencil heavily in the center and blend as shown. *Left leaf:* stencil the edges and blend off; then, using a curved edge of linen, stencil the veins. *Center leaf:* stencil the veins first; then raise this portion of the stencil and shade in the edges. *Rose:* shade the petals as indicated. With a brush, add some fire powder in the center.

PLATE 6 Floated color on stencils and painted foliage. *Left:* the four stenciled units have received floated color. *Top:* the flower, completed in three steps, was first stenciled in solid silver, and when dry, given a wash of alizarin crimson. When this was tacky, the second stencil was applied in silver. *Right:* two treatments of foliage used on stenciled trays.

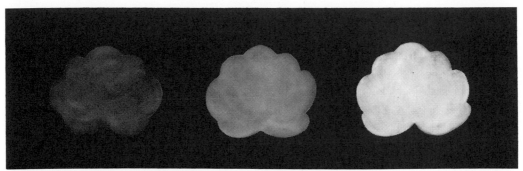

Base coats painted in three degrees of transparency.

Strokes made with a side-loaded brush; these provide good practice for painting petals.

Strokes often used in flower painting.

Overstrokes used for leaves and flowers.

FIGURE 19 *Painting flower parts.*

in the mixture, the edge will bleed. After picking up some paint on the side of the brush, dress it on black paper until it produces the desired blend and value.

The small rose, painted with a few strokes of a side-loaded brush, is not typical of Chippendale painting. However, it is a quick way to get an effect if you are working out a design of your own. Load the brush with the shadow color and drag the side through the desired highlight color. This kind of treatment was actually used on some decorated furniture of the late Victorian period, although it was done with more refinement. Unfortunately, the same method is also used in an assembly-line operation to produce flower decorations on commercial trays. The effect is not very artistic and cannot, of course, be compared to the early handwork.

The strokes in Figure 19(C) are similar to those used in various petal formations. Keep the mixture of paint and varnish a little less than opaque and the stroke will give the illusion of form. Use a square-tipped quill or a pointed red sable such as the Spotter.

In Figure 19(D) combinations of strokes are used to represent veins in leaves and flower parts. Use a No. 2 scroller or a long-pointed No. 1 quill for the long, thin strokes; and a No. 1 scroller for the short ones. All other strokes can be painted with a square-tipped quill or the Spotter.

STEP-BY-STEP FLOWER PAINTING

THE FINISHED paintings (Plates 10 and 11) are copies of flowers found on Chippendale or Gothic trays. The same types of flowers on similar trays may be painted with many variations. If you are able to reproduce these samples you will be able to recognize the procedures used in other treatments. The blue daisy is one of the simplest of Chippendale-type flowers and would be a good one to try first. The colors of any of the flowers can be changed by substituting another color for the one used in the transparent wash. For a white rose, float a greenish wash like the one used for the passion flower. A mixture of transparent yellow and raw or burnt umber (depending on whether you want a warm or cool yellow) will produce a yellow flower (Plate 9). Because artists seldom make two paintings exactly alike, you may find that some of the painted steps vary slightly in outline or arrangement of petals. However, by the time you are ready to try painting flowers, you will have had enough experience to understand the processes and do a little improvising if necessary.

The paint applied in each step should be dry before going on to the next step and, except when otherwise specified, a square-tipped quill, No. 2, No. 3, or No. 5, can be used. When a color or mixture of colors is mentioned, they are to be mixed with varnish—more when thin color is indicated, and less when a heavier or deeper tone is required. Remember that when applying a transparent wash (floating color) over the entire flower, the edges of the flower can be disregarded. The wash can be applied in broad, straight strokes that will cover part of the black background surrounding the flower. If the varnish sets up too fast, a drop or two of linseed oil can be added to it. Blending one color into another necessitates cleaning, wiping, and moistening the brush with varnish, and spreading the tip as wide as possible. If you have trouble with any of the steps, reread the more detailed description of the processes. Always keep a piece of black paper or cardboard near your palette for testing the transparency or blend of a white stroke.

To paint the flowers shown in Plates 10 and 11, follow the directions given below. Trace all flower outlines from Figure 20.

FIGURE 20   *Full-size tracings for Chippendale flowers.*

BLUE DAISY—PLATE 10(A)

1. Paint the semitransparent base coat.
2. Paint the heavier white petals, giving each the proper curve.
3. Float a thin wash of Prussian blue and varnish over the entire flower. Immediately add a stroke of deep blue on the left side and blend it into the paler wash.
4. Paint the green oval center, using the green mixture on the color chart (Plate 1). When dry, add the yellow dots (white and chrome yellow, medium).

BLUE PODS—PLATE 10(B)

1. Paint oval semitransparent base coats.
2. Paint heavier white ovals.
3. Float thinned Prussian blue over the entire oval, then add a heavier stroke on the left side, and blend.
4. Add black dot and yellow dots.

SMALL RED FLOWER—PLATE 10(C)

1. Paint semitransparent base coat.
2. Paint heavier white petals. These can be made as a short straight stroke or two short teardrop strokes.
3. Float a thin wash of alizarin crimson over the flower, paint a heavier stroke on the left side, and blend.
4. Add a thin raw umber circular spot at the center. When dry, paint first a black and then a yellow dot in the center.

WHITE DAISY—PLATE 10(D)

1. Paint the thin white base coat.
2. Paint slightly more opaque white petal formations, leaving the edge of the base coat showing.
3. Before doing this step the flower can be given more of a three-dimensional look by painting another group of slightly whiter strokes just within the ones painted in the last step. Let this dry; then float a thin mixture of Prussian blue, raw umber, and varnish over the entire flower.
4. Add still another layer of white strokes, allowing the edges of those that were colored in Step 3 to show.
5. Paint an oval of alizarin crimson and burnt umber in the center of the flower. Clean the square-tipped quill, moisten in varnish, and spread the tip. Pull out the edges of the oval with the brush, curving the strokes to follow the shapes of the petals. If it doesn't produce the proper fine lines, use a No. 1 scroller to paint the fine lines. When this is dry, paint a black spot in the center and paint yellow and white dots where indicated. Finally, paint a small white stroke on the black dot and strokes of thin burnt sienna on the edges of the petals.

*Reproductions of coffin trays with country
painting. Top tray painted by Annetta Cruze.
Bottom tray painted by Anna Burns. [From
The Decorator]*

PASSION FLOWER—PLATE 10(E)

1–3. The first three steps for the passion flower are exactly the same as those for
the white daisy (Plate 10[D]).

4. Add white highlights on the five larger petals, and thin white strokes to represent turnovers.

5. Paint a *very thin* wash of Prussian blue and alizarin crimson on the turnovers.
Trace the center oval, pistil, and stamens from the outline in Figure 20 and transfer to
the painted flower. It is necessary to place this section in the proper position. Paint

the green oval and the Prussian-blue strokes, using a No. 2 scroller or a No. 1 long-pointed quill for the latter. When these are dry, add the yellow stamens and markings on the pistil, using a No. 2 scroller. Paint the alizarin-crimson strokes around the oval with a scroller or No. 2 Finepoint brush. When these are dry, add the burnt sienna strokes to the stamens. The very fine white lines can be painted with a No. 1 scroller.

MORNING GLORY—PLATE 10(F)

1. Paint the base coat in an almost-opaque white.

2. Paint the yellow area with Indian yellow or yellow lake. Keep the top outline hard, but blend off the bottom portion with clear varnish.

3. Paint a thin wash of Prussian blue over the rest of the flower, blending the bottom area into the yellow. A stroke of clear varnish can be painted on this area before applying the blue wash; this will make blending easier.

4. Paint a stroke of clear varnish in the same area you did in Step 3. Mix a deeper blue mixture and paint the top petal area. Keep the line clean and deep blue where it meets the yellow. Make a large, long crescent stroke with the blue mixture around the bottom of the flower (let it go over onto the background). Quickly clean the quill in turpentine, dry, and moisten with varnish. Spread the tip until it is very wide and pull the blue paint with very light strokes up into the yellow area. Keep the strokes curving in the proper direction. Since this area has already been moistened with clear varnish, the blue strokes should blend partially but still show a few lines. If any part of the other blue area has not blended as it should, stroke it lightly with the widened tip, keeping the strokes going in the general direction of the alizarin crimson over-strokes in the next step. A little linseed oil can be added to the mixture for this step if the paint seems to set up before you have finished working on it.

5. Add the burnt umber stroke in the center. The alizarin crimson strokes should be fairly thin. Use either a square-tipped quill or a pointed red-sable brush such as the Spotter, and start the stroke on the background below the flower. This is one instance where the stroke should not have a nice, clean, pointed tail. Push down at the edge of the petal and feather off, or lift the brush quickly as you curve in towards the center. With a No. 1 scroller, paint the fine red lines around the bottom edge with King Cole orange or cadmium red, light. Paint the funnel of the flower with clear varnish and add a stroke of alizarin crimson and burnt umber on the side, letting it float into the clear varnish. When this is dry, add the green sepal.

FUCHSIA—PLATE 10(G)

1. Paint the base coat in semitransparent white.

2. Add heavier white accents.

3. Float a deep wash of alizarin crimson and varnish over the entire flower.

4. Add orange-red accents.

5. Add blue strokes (white, Prussian blue, and alizarin crimson) and orange-red stamens.

ROSE—PLATE 11 (A)

1. Paint the base coat in semitransparent white.

2. Float a thin wash of alizarin crimson with a little burnt umber over the entire base coat. Immediately after doing this, pick up more of the color and paint deeper strokes where indicated.

3. While the paint used in Step 2 is still wet, lightly stroke the color until the darker tones blend somewhat into the thin wash.

4. Paint the small brush strokes in thin white; then with a side-loaded brush, paint the first layer of petals.

5. Paint the second layer of petals.

6. Paint the third layer of petals on the cup section and the outer petals, which must curve toward the imaginary spot at the base of the cup. Add the alizarin-crimson strokes when the white petals are dry.

ROSE—PLATE 11 (B)

1. Paint the base coat in thin white.

2. With a slightly heavier white, paint only the cup section, leaving some of the base coat showing at the top. While it is still wet, paint some heavier white strokes on the outer area of the cup, and blend. Side-load the brush with white and paint the outer petals.

3. Float a thin wash of alizarin crimson with a little yellow lake or Indian yellow over the entire flower. Pick up more alizarin crimson and paint heavy strokes in the center and around the base of the cup, and blend into the thin wash.

4. Side-load the brush with white paint (not too heavy) and paint the inside petals. Paint the first layer of petals on the outer edge of the cup.

5. Paint the second layer of petals in the same way.

6. Paint the third layer of petals. If necessary, on the large petal in the middle, more white can be added and blended at the same time, or later. Paint the petals in the outer layer as in Step 2, keeping them thin on the left side. Add white accents and alizarin-crimson strokes. When this layer is dry, a *very thin* wash of Prussian blue with Indian yellow, or alizarin crimson with Prussian blue, can be painted on the left side of the cup and the right side of the inner layer of petals. This gives more of a shadow effect. Paint yellow dots.

ROSE—PLATE 11 (C)

1. Paint the thin white base coat.

2. With a side-loaded brush paint the first group of petals.

3. Paint the next group of petals.

4. Paint the next group of petals. Where two overlap, you may have to wait an hour or two before doing the last one.

5. Paint the final group of petals.

75]

6. Paint a wash of clear varnish over the entire flower. While wet, paint a stroke of alizarin crimson with a little Indian yellow and burnt umber over the top petals and on the left side. Blend this well into the clear varnish and then add a spot of deeper red in the center. A stroke of thinned color can be painted around the base, as indicated, after the original wash has dried somewhat.

ABOVE. *Reproduction of stenciled box. Stenciled by Louise Wallace.* BELOW: *Reproduction of* *tin trunk. Painted by Helen Spear.* [*From* The Decorator]

[76

VII

Lace-Edge Painting

Lace-edge painting gets its name from the round, oval, and oblong trays with pierced, lacelike rims on which this style of painting was most often used. (For this and other types of trays, see Figure 21.) These trays appeared in about the same period as the Gothic or Chippendale trays. They were first produced in Pontypool, Wales, along with other articles, such as baskets, teapots, and urns, which bore the same type of design. The trays were usually painted black or given an imitation tortoise-shell background. The favorite subjects for decoration were fruit and flowers. An urn with swag and accompanying foliage was also a popular design, and occasionally one finds a figure or coat of arms used as decoration. On round trays the center design was often circled with wreaths, ribbons, or clusters of small flowers, and borders on the floors were delicate, gold-leaf designs in line or stroke.

This style of painting seems to resemble canvas painting more than the other techniques. The paint itself contributes to the form as much as does the stroke and the color. Ridgy strokes create highlights which contrast sharply with deep, transparent shadows. The formula for the painting medium used to produce this impasto effect has never been accurately determined. However, the wax medium, or Master Medium, which is used, makes it possible to get just these effects, and since it is based on formulas used by some of the Old Masters, it could be similar to the original.

77]

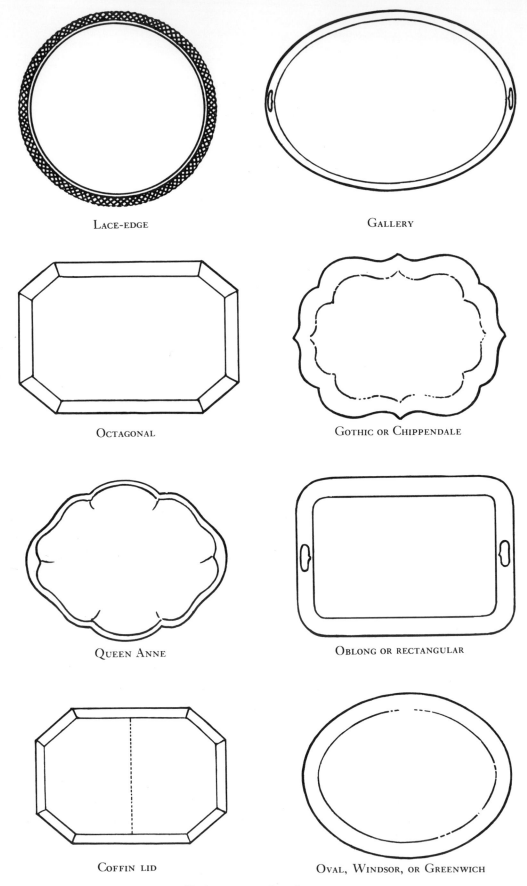

LACE-EDGE

GALLERY

OCTAGONAL

GOTHIC OR CHIPPENDALE

QUEEN ANNE

OBLONG OR RECTANGULAR

COFFIN LID

OVAL, WINDSOR, OR GREENWICH

FIGURE 21 *Various types of antique trays.*
On gallery, Gothic, and oblong trays a Chinese
influence was often evident.

LACE-EDGE *Round (sometimes with unpierced edge), oval, and oblong.* Decoration: *painting and gold leaf, usually of flowers or fruit.*

GALLERY *Always oval with solid or cut-out "keyhole" rim.* Decoration: *gold leaf, often with single or double borders with painted accents. Painted scenes, portrait medallions, and sometimes flower paintings similar to those on lace-edge trays.*

OCTAGONAL *Wide flange.* Decoration: *gold leaf and freehand bronze in center designs; or, more often, single or double borders. Occasionally painted scenes or portrait medallions.*

GOTHIC OR CHIPPENDALE *Metal or papier-mâché.* Decoration: *gold leaf, freehand bronze, and painting; borders alone or with center designs including scenes, flowers, birds, and fountains. Occasionally one-piece stencils on small, sharp-edged trays.*

QUEEN ANNE Decoration: *gold leaf with painted flowers (Chippendale type).*

OBLONG OR RECTANGULAR *With or without handholes.* Decoration: *stenciling, freehand bronze, and gold leaf, alone or combined in single or double borders, pictorial center designs, fruit, or flowers. Painted scenes and Chippendale-flower painting.*

COFFIN LID *Octagonal, with narrow flange. Sometimes seamed.* Decoration: *country painting and occasionally a one-piece stencil.*

OVAL, WINDSOR, OR GREENWICH *Oval with rounded edge.* Decoration: *early trays had gold leaf used alone or combined with Chippendale-flower painting and, occasionally, mother-of-pearl inlay. Later trays bore simple gold-leaf and painted borders.*

SUPPLIES AND EQUIPMENT

Wax Medium   This is a jellylike substance which is sold in tubes under the name Master Medium. A few paint companies are producing something similar, such as Grumbacher's Gel, but I prefer the Master Medium, which is available at the address listed under "Suppliers," (page 238).

FIGURE 22   *Stroke exercises for lace-edge painting.*

As a substitute for varnish, the wax medium is satisfying to work with because it dries very slowly and eliminates the pressure to get finished before the paint is really dry. For this reason it is an excellent medium to use when painting scenic or portrait designs. It can be blended easily, and also produces crisp overstrokes on the final painting; however, wax medium reduces covering quality of paints, and because of this, base coats are generally painted with a mixture of paint and varnish.

Before the finishing coats of varnish are applied, trays which are painted with a mixture of paint and wax medium must be allowed to dry much longer than those on which a mixture of paint and varnish has been used. Patterns can be varnished when there is still a slight tack; but when several coats of varnish are to be used, the painting should not be touched for several weeks prior to their application.

STROKE EXERCISES FOR LACE-EDGE PAINTING

FIGURE 22 shows a variety of basic strokes that might be found on a lace-edge tray design; they are painted with a mixture of white in japan colors and the wax medium. Notice that they are quite different from the strokes used in Chippendale painting. The paint is ridgy and these ridges actually contribute to the design. The quill brush that has been used for most of the other painting is not satisfactory for this work because it has so little resistance to pressure. The Spotter (No. 4) and a scroller (No. 2) were used for the practice strokes, but any red-sable watercolor brush that is not too fine at the point could be substituted for the Spotter.

1. Squeeze about ½ teaspoon of wax medium onto your palette, and using a palette knife, mix a little of it with some striping white in japan. Work some of the medium into your brush and dip the tip into the white paint. *Do not dress the brush.*

2. Holding the brush almost perpendicular, push the tip down on the black paper until about one-half the length of the hair is flat. Pull the brush first toward you and then up, as you would for any brush stroke. If the paint is too thin, pick up a little more white. If it is too solid, use more medium in the brush. Sometimes the second stroke—without reloading—is a better consistency. It will take some practice to discover the proper proportion of paint and medium for the various strokes. If strokes are not satisfactory, wipe them off. It is not possible to doctor them at all, since the freedom and authority with which the stroke is painted determine the quality of the work.

PAINTING LACE-EDGE FLOWERS AND LEAVES

THE ROSE in Plate 12 is created in four basic steps which are used for other examples, both simple and elaborate. Sometimes the base coat is white instead of red, or the veiling mixture in Step 3 is slightly different in color and consistency. More white or some alizarin crimson may be added. Always remember to rub (I use

FIGURE 23 *Full-size tracings for lace-edge* *sprays are not included, as they should be* *units. The white overstrokes on the flower* *painted freehand.*

my finger) some wax medium over a varnished surface before adding strokes which are a mixture of paint and the medium. If this is not done, the paint mixture tends to "crawl" and the strokes will not hold their shape. The strokes used for the small daisylike flowers are similar to the first groups in the stroke exercises. Half of the

81]

petals are often white; and the other half are blue, or red, or two shades of either color. Tracings for lace-edge units are found in Figure 23.

ROSE—PLATE 12

1. Paint the base coat in orange in japan, or cadmium red, light, in oil color, and varnish. Notice that its outline is usually well within the outline of the finished flower.

2. When the base coat is dry, float thin alizarin crimson and varnish over the entire flower, and add heavier alizarin crimson in the center and around the bottom of the cup as indicated.

3. Rub some wax medium over the entire flower when it has dried. For this rose, mix some orange-red with a very small amount of white and burnt umber. Add a small amount of wax medium and mix throughly with your palette knife. Work some of the medium into your brush as you did for the stroke exercises, and pick up the color on the tip. Test the consistency on black paper and when the mixture is right, paint the strokes around and beyond the edges of the base coat.

4. This step will take longer to dry than those painted with varnish. It might be wise on the first attempt to allow Step 3 to dry for perhaps a week. Give it a coat of varnish, and when this is dry, paint the final white petals. By doing this you will be able to wipe off any unsatisfactory petals and repaint them. Mix a little orange-red with the white for these petals. They can be painted consecutively, unlike the Chippendale type which have to dry before the succeeding layers are added. Always paint first the petals which are partially covered by another layer, and finish with the outer layer of petals. Add the alizarin crimson and orange-red strokes where indicated.

LEAVES—PLATE 12

The painted leaves on lace-edge trays were generally a blue-green with blended highlights and crisp overstrokes. Occasionally a base coat of orange-red was painted and allowed to dry before adding the greens. In this case the green paint was thinned in spots to allow the red to show through faintly. Small leaves were edged with yellowish white strokes.

1. Mix some Prussian blue, raw umber, and wax medium, and paint the entire leaf with this mixture. You will barely be able to see it.

2. Clean the brush, pick up some white and yellow ochre, and paint the areas indicated. If it seems too bright, add a little raw umber.

3. Use either a bright's red-sable brush, No. 6 or 8, or the pointed red sable you have been using spread at the tip, and blend the light strokes into the dark background.

4. Paint the veins with black enamel or seal, and the light strokes with a mixture of white, yellow ochre, and wax medium. This step can be done at once or you can let the leaf dry and varnish it before adding the overstrokes.

PART TWO

APPLYING THE

TECHNIQUES

PLATE 7 Typical freehand-bronze units. *Rose:* make silver strokes with a stump. Using a bob, apply fire and silver powder on outer petals; when dry, float alizarin crimson and Indian yellow in center and the outer edge of the cup. When dry, add alizarin crimson and burnt-umber overstrokes, and white dots. *Pomegranate:* use a bob and brush for deep-gold strokes, and velvet and a brush for blending the highlight out to the edge. *Peach:* bronze as indicated, and when dry, float alizarin crimson and burnt umber, separately, on the right and left sections. Add strokes and dots.

Shell: apply rich-gold powder and blend to the edges. Paint the opening with striping white. When dry, float alizarin crimson and burnt umber over the white. Add the burnt-umber strokes, yellow dots, and black lines. *Strawberries:* apply silver powder. When dry, float shaded alizarin crimson and Indian yellow. Allow to dry, then add black and white dots. *Small leaves:* apply rich and deep gold. Add black veins. *Large leaf:* make small silver strokes with a stump and blend rich gold from the edges toward the center. Add burnt-umber strokes and black veins.

PLATE 8   Etching on metal leaf. *Top, left to right:* metal-leaf samples of XX gold, lemon gold, pale gold, and palladium. *Left rose:* etched in realistic style with dry brush, burnt-umber shading. *Center rose:* single etching and side-loaded floated color (alizarin crimson and burnt umber). *Daisy:* drawn with single etcher; shaded with triple etcher. *Leaf:* has single-etched lines; a thin, burnt-umber stroke; and black vein. *Scroll:* is typical of a Chippendale border. *Design, lower right:* includes stormont work.

VIII

Preparation of Tin and Wood

THE PREPARATION and finishing of a decorated article are extremely important steps that reveal the decorator's craftsmanship as much as does the painted decoration. Each layer of paint must be perfectly smooth before the next layer is applied; it is impossible to cover up poor work with succeeding layers. There seem to be no shortcuts to this part of the decorating process, although some reproductions and new tin are available already painted and ready to decorate, which eliminates the first operation.

The majority of the old trays, boxes, etc., were painted black, which made an effective background for the painting, stenciling, and gold leaf used in the decoration. Red was probably the next most popular color while other colors were more rarely used. Trays with white backgrounds and delicate designs in gold leaf and color were referred to as brides' trays.

Many shiny-tin country pieces were painted with transparent colors which produced lively backgrounds for primitive painting and stenciling. The most popular finish was black asphaltum which produces a coppery color if it is not applied too heavily. The tin must be very shiny to get the proper effect. Transparent reds, blues, and greens were also used.

White, gold, or sometimes red bands were used as backgrounds for parts of the design. On Chippendale and oblong trays the black background was sometimes dusted with bronze powder shaded from the center to the flange, or less often from the edge to the center, which gave the effect of a gold background.

85]

The treatment of backgrounds on furniture and smaller wooden articles varied according to the period and location. Chairs were painted in solid colors ranging from black, dark reds, and greens, to white and color tints. The white was occasionally smoked, rarely on chairs, but quite often on bellows and bands. The old decorators were specialists in the art of imitation and the most extensive application of this art was in the practice of wood graining. In modern furniture such an imitation would not be acceptable to anyone who is looking for quality, but because of its antiquity, and in most cases the skill with which it was handled, imitation woodgrains are regarded with respect. In fact, decorators make every effort to produce expert imitations of the imitations.

On most chairs, such as the popular Hitchcock, the graining was done to give the effect of rosewood, harewood, or other precious woods. The rosewood effect was obtained by painting a thin black over a rusty-red background. It is said that at the old Hitchcock factory in Riverton, Connecticut, part of the equipment was a large tank filled with water into which were thrown all kinds of scrap iron from nails, horseshoes, etc., to the worn-out rims of wagon wheels. The disintegration of the iron imparted a red color to the water and acted as a dye on the wooden chair parts which were immersed in it. Some chairs are so beautifully grained that they actually resemble the precious woods and are usually decorated only with striping. Another type of graining was called either stale-ale, or putty graining. This type is found mostly on chair seats and chests; it is now used effectively on boxes, sometimes by substituting ingredients which are more easily obtained.

Supplies and Equipment

Articles to Decorate   It is getting harder and harder to find antique tinware that is not prohibitively priced. If you do acquire a decorated original, it would be wise to consult an expert before doing anything to it. Many pieces should be restored or left in their original state rather than stripped and redecorated, and it is difficult for a beginner to know which course to follow. The design can always be recorded and reproduced on another article.

Reproductions of almost all types of antique trays and some boxes can be found. Most stores which carry decorating supplies either have these in stock or can order them. There are also a number of shapes which are not exact copies of antiques, but which can be decorated with the old designs or adaptations.

Primer and Paints   Red sanding primer, flat black, black asphaltum, and Venetian red in japan are satisfactory in a number of brands; therefore no specific one is especially recommended. Pittsburgh's DeRusto or Rustoleum, which come in white, can be used in place of red sanding primer under light colors.

All paints and varnishes should be smooth and free from lumps. Unless a new can of paint is being used, it is a good idea to strain the paint or varnish through a nylon stocking into a container before applying. To strain a small amount quickly,

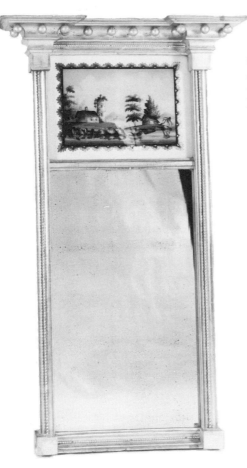

Gilded mirror frame withnted pai glass. Owned by HSEAD, Inc. [Courtesy of the Farmer's Museum, Cooperstown, New York]

Mirror with painted glass. Owned by Mrs. Wasimir. [From The Decorator]

secure a piece of nylon stocking over the can with an elastic band and push the center of it below the paint level. The paint that appears above the stocking is automatically strained.

Sandpaper Wet-or-dry sandpaper is a dark gray color and comes in several different grit sizes. The finest is No. 600, which sometimes seems too fine to remove bumps on varnished surfaces; but it is less likely to scratch than No. 500. To smooth the sanding primer, No. 400 can be used wet. This type of sandpaper is sold under several brand names, two of which are Tri-M-ite Wetordry and Jewellite Waterproof.

Brushes   The best brush with which to apply the *background* paints is an ox-hair brush, ¾ to 1 inch, depending on the size of the article. Since it is so important to have every coat of paint on an article as smooth as possible, it is necessary to have an adequate brush. This brush should be wiped to remove the paint, then rinsed in turpentine, and finally washed with soap and water before storing.

White Pencil   There are many different brands of white pencils but not all of them will produce a mark on a varnished or shiny surface. One of the most effective is produced by J. S. Staedtler, Inc. (see "Suppliers," page 239.) Others on the market are: Eagle Prismacolor, No. 938; Faber, No. 2388; and Blaisdell.

Lithopone Powder   Lithopone is a fine, white, chalky powder that is available wherever decorating supplies are sold.

Paraffin Oil   See Chapter X.

Restoring Antique Tin

Some antiques which are in fair condition are much more decorative and also more valuable if left alone. As previously mentioned, if you find a piece of decorated tin, get the advice of an expert before you strip or repaint it. To restore it, do the following:

1. Try washing the article with detergent and warm water to remove the surface dirt. Rub carefully with a moistened cloth and Lava soap. A stronger treatment would be alternate applications of alcohol and turpentine, ending with the turpentine. Work very carefully, using a different cloth for the application of each liquid. The strongest cleaner is a solution of equal parts of alcohol and acetone. This should be used only if the other methods fail to produce results. Again, rub very carefully, and if some of the color from the decoration appears on the cloth, let it rest for awhile before continuing. A stencil knife can be used to scrape off stubborn spots of discolored varnish or shellac.

2. When all the dirt has been removed and the design seems to be showing its original color, fill in any breaks in the surface with a mixture of sanding primer and lithopone. (See Step 4 under "Old Tin II," page 90.)

3. When this is dry, sand the spots well with wet-or-dry No. 400 sandpaper dipped in water. Let dry, and give the article a coat of varnish.

4. After the varnish is thoroughly dry, paint in the background color where it is missing. Matching a black background is sometimes tricky; try adding raw umber to the black paint.

5. When the background paint is dry, repaint the sections of design that are missing and finish as described under "Finishing," Chapter X.

[*88*

Lace-edge tray with tortoise-shell background, painted fruit, and gold-leaf border. From the *Mrs. Arthur Oldham collection.* [*From* The Ornamented Tray]

OLD TIN I—WHEN DESIGN IS WORTH RECORDING

1. Remove all dirt from the article, using as strong a solution as necessary. (See above, "Restoring Antique Tin.")

2. Let the article dry thoroughly, then give it a coat of clear varnish which will bring out the design.

3. Allow to dry thoroughly and trace around the fainter units with a sharp white pencil or with a No. 1 scroller and white paint.

4. Lay a piece of acetate over the design, tape it down, and trace the outlines with pen and ink. If the design continues from the floor of a tray onto the flange, it is easier to hold the acetate in place by cutting two small squares near the center and taping it through these, leaving the part over the flange untaped.

5. A complete color record of the design should be made either on acetate or cardboard, following the directions for whichever technique had been used on the article.

6. When the design has been carefully recorded, strip and prepare the article as described under "Old Tin II," below.

OLD TIN II—WHEN NO DESIGN IS VISIBLE

Again, consult an expert before stripping a piece of antique tin which shows no decoration or such a small portion that it would seem impossible to restore. Most of the old designs were repeated many times, and your piece may include a design which had been partially recorded. However, the consultant may advise that the design was not worth recording, since it was a poor example of that particular period. If this is the case, or if there seems to be no possibility of finding a design under the background paint, use the following procedure for stripping.

1. Following directions on the can, remove all the old paint with paint remover.

2. After all the old paint has been removed and the tin smoothed with sandpaper, apply Rust-i-cide, following the directions on the bottle, if there is any rust on the piece.

3. When thoroughly dry, paint with metal primer (red sanding primer.)

4. If the article is badly pitted, fill the holes with lithopone powder and sanding primer mixed to the consistency of paste. Smooth off with a palette knife.

5. After this is dry, sand well with fine garnet paper. Apply as many coats of the primer as are necessary to make the surface reasonably level. Wait twenty-four hours between coats.

6. When thoroughly dry, sand the article until very smooth with either wet-or-dry No. 400 sandpaper dipped in water, or a very fine garnet paper.

Stenciled walls in bridal chamber of Weston Farmhouse, Temple, New Hampshire. At- *tributed to Moses Eaton. Owned by Mrs. Wilfred Weston. [From* The Decorator]

New Tin

1. Wash the article with hot water and detergent to remove the grease or oil. It can also be wiped with cider vinegar.

2. Follow Steps 3, 5, and 6 under "Old Tin II," above.

Wood

1. New wood or old wood from which all the old finish has been removed with paint remover or sanding can be given a coat of red sanding primer and sanded smooth if it is to be painted *black* or a *dark color*. If it is to be painted a *light color*, it can be first painted with a flat white or a tint. If it is to be left *natural*, it should be given a coat of shellac thinned with alcohol before it is decorated. Any of these base coats should be sanded before starting the decoration.

Wood that is to be decorated can be prepared quickly by rubbing Hour Varnish into the wood with a nylon stocking. This would be practical, however, only for small articles such as breadboards, boxes, etc. To get an antiqued effect on the background before decorating, rub the wood first with paraffin oil, then with raw and/or burnt umber until the desired shade is obtained.

Opaque Backgrounds

BLACK

1. Mix flat-black paint in the can until it is well blended. It is usually fairly thick, so it should be thinned with turpentine until it looks like black ink. Two or three thin coats of paint will give a much smoother finish than one thick coat. Using a ½ to 1 inch ox-hair brush, paint the article, starting with the flange or rim if it is a tray. The first coat need not cover perfectly because one or two more coats should be applied, allowing twenty-four hours between coats.

2. When dry, rub with No. 0000 steel wool if the surface seems at all rough. Now it is ready for decoration. The matte surface is easy to work on, but its disadvantage is that corrections are difficult to make without affecting the background. It is better, especially for beginners, to give the article a coat of varnish (see "Finishing," Chapter X) and rub the gloss off with steel wool. Always be sure that all particles of the steel wool have been wiped off the article before continuing on to the next step. On this varnished surface, it is possible to remove errors, if the paint is still wet, with either a dry cloth or one moistened with varnish, Energine, or turpentine. (Try in this order.)

COLOR

There are many prepared paints available in beautiful shades such as the Williamsburg colors. Most paint stores mix colors to order from sample chips. If you wish to mix tints yourself, add small amounts of tube oil colors to flat or semi-gloss white. Venetian red, added to white, produces a soft peach pink. Veridian and white make a clear aqua shade and a little Vandyke brown added to white gives a warm gray tone. These colors are not in your basic lists but are easily obtained in small tubes. For darker colors, pick a prepared paint nearest to the shade you want, and add tube colors to change it. Umbers, black, or the complement of the original color will tone it down. Chrome yellow added to black makes a nice antique green with an olive tone. Use a light-colored metal primer under the lightest background paints to cut down on the number of layers of paint necessary to cover.

TRANSPARENT BACKGROUNDS

TRANSPARENT background colors have to be applied over very shiny tin to create the proper effect. If it is necessary to use a transparent paint and the antique piece cannot be made shiny, give it a coat of varnish and when tacky, rub silver or aluminum bronze powder over the entire surface. When dry, wash with mild soap and water, and then varnish again; let dry before applying the transparent paint. This method of imitating shiny tin is never quite as satisfactory as using the real thing.

ASPHALTUM

1. Mix a little black asphaltum into some gloss varnish. The amount will depend on the shade desired. Try a bit of the mixture on a tin can to test it. Asphaltum varnish can also be used and lightened by adding more varnish.

A substitute for asphaltum which seems to come closest to its color is a mixture of one part mahogany varnish stain to two parts walnut varnish stain.

2. Moisten a cloth with turpentine and wipe over the surface; then paint with the asphaltum mixture, using an ox-hair brush. Set aside to dry but check for drips.

3. Allow to dry thoroughly or bake in an oven set at 250 degrees for about a half hour. Don't bake the article if it is an antique, however, for the heat will melt the solder.

4. Varnish the article and allow to dry before decorating.

TRANSPARENT RED

Mix some alizarin crimson with varnish. A combination of asphaltum and alizarin crimson makes a beautiful color.

TRANSPARENT BLUE

Mix Prussian blue with varnish.

Early stenciled turtleback chair with Directoire legs. Owned by H. H. Ferris. [From The Ornamented Chair]

TRANSPARENT GREEN

Mix Indian yellow with Prussian blue and add varnish.

SMOKED BACKGROUNDS

WHITE BACKGROUNDS and bands were sometimes smoked before being decorated. While the white paint is still wet, hold the article over a smoking candle (try holding it horizontally). Move it about in several directions to create different patterns. This will take some experimenting. When the paint is dry, varnish the article and let it dry before decorating.

BRONZED BACKGROUNDS

1. Varnish a black background.

2. When this is tacky—about the same as for stenciling—pick up a 3 or 4 inch square of lamb's wool or fur and fold back the four corners so that no edge will touch the tray. Mouton and otter fur are also excellent for this process, and may be available from a furrier.

3. Holding the fur pad by the corners, pick up some bronze powder of the shade used in the middle. Apply this powder in the bright center area, using a rotary motion but not much pressure. Go over the same spot many times with a light touch until the desired luster is produced. Slowly work out from the center and blend the powder into the black background as indicated.

4. If two or more shades of bronze powder are used, blend the first shade out for an inch or so. Pick up some of the second shade—this might be a deep gold or copper—and *starting back in the center*, rub lightly with a rotary motion in the already bronzed area and beyond, blending out to nothing. There should be a very slight resistance as you work out. If you feel no resistance at all, the varnish may be too dry. If this is the case, let it dry completely, wash with mild soap and water, wipe well, and revarnish.

5. If a third shade such as fire bronze powder is evident at the outer edge of the bronzed area, repeat Step 4 again, starting in the center and lightening the pressure as you blend off into the black background. Sometimes a large, soft, camel-hair brush is helpful for blending.

6. Occasionally the bronzed background starts at the edge of the flange and blends off toward the center. The same method would be used, although in the examples I have seen, the blending looked more like wide brush strokes and the powder extended in some spots behind the center design.

7. When the varnish is dry, wash the tray with mild soap and water, dry carefully, and varnish again before decorating.

TORTOISE-SHELL BACKGROUNDS

USED OCCASIONALLY on lace-edge trays, this process produces a more interesting background than the solid black.

1. After preparing the tray with a black background as previously described under "Opaque Backgrounds," dust the surface lightly with talcum powder, and paint three or four uneven patches in gold size or varnish.

2. When this is tacky, apply palladium leaf. (See directions for laying metal leaf in Chapter V.)

3. At least twenty-four hours later, after removing the loose leaf, paint the

tray with a mixture of alizarin crimson and varnish. It should be a quite brilliant red.

4. Wait twenty-four hours, or more if necessary (alizarin crimson dries slowly), and give the tray a coat of asphaltum varnish, asphaltum mixed with varnish, or the substitute for asphaltum mentioned under "Transparent Backgrounds."

5. While this coat is still wet, pat the areas where the leaf was applied with a crumpled cloth to show up more of the red undercoat in a design effect. Try not to expose any of the hard edges of the leaf patches. When this has dried *thoroughly*, give the tray a coat of varnish, allow to dry, and rub with No. 0000 steel wool before starting the decoration.

ROSEWOOD GRAINING

1. Mix Venetian red in japan with turpentine and a few drops of varnish to a fairly thin consistency.

2. Paint a coat of this mixture over the priming coat used on the wood.

3. When this coat is thoroughly dry (it takes several days), mix flat black with turpentine to a very thin consistency.

4. Paint a small area with the thin black and immediately, using either an old, rather stiff 1-inch brush or a piece of crumpled newspaper, wipe out strips of black by pressing rather hard on the surface and dragging the brush or paper down or across in a wavy line. Keep the wavy lines fairly parallel, but vary them a bit to give the effect of graining. If the graining is being done on a chair, leave the slat to be decorated solid black.

5. A coat of dark-oak varnish stain can be applied when Step 4 is dry to give it a deeper reddish glow.

TONGUE-OF-FLAME GRAINING

THE OLD method usually used on wooden chair seats called for the use of glue size, sugar, and vinegar, but it is possible to use the same materials used in the rosewood graining by reversing the colors. Paint strokes of red over the black background, using an old bristle brush from which some bristles have been cut in uneven lengths.

STALE-ALE OR PUTTY GRAINING

1. First paint the object with flat paint in a light color. Chair seats were usually painted in a light yellow ochre and grained with brown. This gave the effect of oak. Very lovely combinations for chests or boxes are light reds, blues, and greens grained in darker shades of the same color.

2. When the paint is dry, rub the object with vinegar.

3. Stale ale, which was originally used for this process, had both drying and adhesive qualities. However, vinegar with a sweetener added seems to be a good substitute. Dissolve ½ teaspoon of sugar (or use a few drops of maple or sugar syrup)

in two tablespoons of vinegar and add dry pigment of the desired color until the mixture resembles a thin paint.

4. Brush this paint over the area to be grained and proceed immediately with the graining process.

5. Many common materials, such as crumpled cloth or paper, putty, feathers, or old bristle brushes, were used to create the grained effect. When using putty, manipulate a piece of a convenient size and pat the object to produce symmetrical impressions. Change the shape of the putty to change the design, patting it on a paper towel periodically to remove excess paint. To get the shell effect that was often used in the corners of chests, roll the putty to form a cylinder. Hold one end of the roll in one corner of the area and rotate the other end around in a circular direction, lifting it and rolling it so that the marks fanning out from the center create the appearance of a shell. There are endless possibilities for designs, so some experimenting might be quite rewarding.

IX

Applying the Decoration

STUDENTS OFTEN ASK, "How do you get the picture on the tray?" Many of them have a mental image of the pattern being cut out and glued to the article with the edges mysteriously disappearing—and some may feel it is unfortunate that this is not so! After painting a design on a flat piece of acetate, producing the same design on a tray or on a six-sided box may seem to present a problem. Here are a few tips on how to apply decorations to various objects.

SUPPLIES AND EQUIPMENT

White Pencil　See Chapter VIII.

Transfer Papers　Transfer papers that produce a white line are usually made as explained under "Tracing on Dark Backgrounds," page 100. Graphite paper is a thin, dark-gray paper, slightly glossier on one side. The very best quality is called Saral. It comes in graphite as well as in several colors, and the lines can be removed easily without smudging. Manufactured by S. B. Albertis, 5 Tudor City Place, New York, New York 10017.

Striping Brushes　There are two kinds of striping brushes. One is called a *sword*, or *dagger*, striper; and the other is a 2-inch *quill*, sometimes called a *rattail* striper. The former is shaped like a sword and comes in several sizes, although it is possible to paint stripes of various widths with one size, since width is determined by the position of the brush and the amount of pressure exerted. Another advantage is that the sword, or dagger, striper holds more paint and does not have to be reloaded as often. The rattail striper also comes in different sizes, but the width of the stripes painted by each one depends on loading and dressing the brush. There are devotees of both kinds, but the rattail seems to be easier for the beginner to handle.

Rottenstone   Rottenstone is a very fine, dark-gray powder used in polishing. It is available at paint or art supply stores.

PAINTING POSITIONS

IT IS A good idea to first decorate the floor of a tray unless the flange (rim) has already been decorated and then varnished. Working on the floor presents no problem, but when painting the flange, the tray must be held so that there is good light and the painting hand is supported either against the floor or the edge of the flange. Large trays can be held in the lap and balanced against a table.

Round or cylindrical objects and boxes can be held in place and supported with weights or heavy objects. Weights such as those used in old-time scales or clocks are useful additions to your equipment. Weights can also be used for holding pieces of tracing paper or palette paper, and for holding two materials which are being glued together.

It is easier to stencil a chair splat when the chair is placed on a tabletop and rested on its back. When decorating several chairs in the same manner, line them up across a long table and do one step on all of them in an assembly-line operation, before going on to the next process. You will be stenciling the design upside down, but you can prop the pattern (also upside down) against the chair seat, which will act as an easel. Striping on a horizontal surface is easier; and after the stiles, splats, legs, etc., are striped, the chair can be set up on its legs for striping the seat. It is better to stripe and paint long, fine strokes from a standing position. In this position, your hand and arm have more freedom of movement.

A good support for large pieces of furniture such as chests, tables, settees, etc., is an old, round dining table with the legs cut to a convenient height—mine is 18 inches high. Put casters on the table for ease in moving.

WHITE BANDS

ON SOME country-tin pieces the design was painted on a white or semi-transparent band which had been added over the background color. Coffin trays with Pennsylvania German designs often had white bands on the tray floors; tin trunks as well were frequently decorated in this manner. White bands occasionally appear as backgrounds for freehand-bronze borders.

1. Measure and draw guidelines for the placement of the band on the tray. This can be done most efficiently by using a compass with a white pencil. When drawing lines on the floor of a tray, balance the point of the compass against the

[98

9 9]

turn—the place where the floor meets the flange—of the tray, and then adjust the compass so that the pencil hits the proper banding width. Pull the compass around the tray, concentrating on the point to make sure it doesn't leave the groove, and letting the pencil touch the floor lightly. If the sharp metal point of the compass scratches the varnished surface, wrap a small piece of adhesive tape over the point. If the guidelines for the band are on the flange of the tray, balance the point of the compass over the edge and then adjust the compass pencil properly. On a tin trunk the point of the compass can be held against the ridge under the cover.

2. Use prepared flat-white paint or striping white in japan for the band. In either case add enough raw umber to produce a slightly "dirty" white. Thin either mixture with turpentine and a few drops of varnish until it is of the right consistency. Use a ½ to 1 inch ox-hair brush or a No. 5 square-tipped quill (depending on the width of the band), but before painting the article, paint a few strokes on a piece of black paper until you get the desired effect. The painted band should be smooth and have a translucent appearance, with the background showing through very slightly.

3. When the band is dry, varnish and allow to dry before decorating.

Gold Bands

WIDE BANDS in bronze powder or gold leaf were often used on rectangular trays on either the flange or both the flange and the floor. The decoration on these bands was generally done in freehand bronze alone, or in combination with painting. When the band appeared only on the flange, it was occasionally decorated with white or black line combinations, such as crosshatching, thereby producing the effect of a picture frame.

1. Measure and draw guidelines, as explained in Step 1 under "White Bands."

2. Using the proper ox-hair brush or square-tipped quill, paint the band with varnish or with a mixture of varnish and enough yellow enamel to show on the background. Try to keep the edges as straight as possible, although this type of band was usually striped on either side to straighten the edges. If it is a large tray, paint in both directions from the first stroke. This will allow the first stroke to blend with the final strokes.

3. When the band is tacky—as for stenciling or gold leafing—either rub bronze powder firmly onto the varnish and polish well, and wash when dry or lay gold leaf, as described in Chapter V. Always varnish the band before decorating.

Transferring the Tracing to an Article

TRACING ON DARK BACKGROUNDS

1. Make a transfer sheet by rubbing lithopone powder firmly on a piece of tracing paper; then wipe off the loose powder. For a more permanent tracing used for larger designs, first dampen the paper with turpentine, and while it is still damp, rub in the powder. For small designs or tracings you do not wish to keep, the powder can

be rubbed on the back of the tracing rather than on a separate piece of tracing paper.

2. Place the tracing in the proper position on the varnished article and secure it with masking tape.

3. If the tracing itself has not been treated, slip the transfer sheet, *treated side down*, between the tracing and the article, and trace all the lines with a stylus or very hard No. 8H pencil. Since the transfer sheet can be moved around under the tracing, it need not be the size of the pattern. Before tracing too much, check to see that the lines show clearly.

Do as little tracing as possible. This eliminates the necessity of cleaning off tracing lines which have not been covered. It is never necessary to trace any overstrokes since the base coat, when painted, would cover the tracing. Do not trace squiggles, swirls, or any strokes which depend on freedom of execution for success; following a tracing line would make them appear stilted. It is better to trace small brush strokes with one line that shows position and direction rather than to outline them completely.

TRACING ON LIGHT BACKGROUNDS

Be sure that the light background has been varnished and made dull with powdered pumice before tracing. Graphite paper can be used for transferring designs onto light backgrounds. Slip the paper, glossy side down, under the tracing.

A transfer sheet can be made by substituting colored chalk for the lithopone powder.

If neither of these materials is available, go over the outlines on the back of the tracing with a soft lead pencil; then place the tracing on the article, penciled side down, and go over the lines again with a stylus or hard pencil. Sometimes just rubbing over the lines with your thumbnail will provide enough of an outline to work from. Whichever method is used, do not make heavy tracing lines—they are sometimes hard to remove from a light-colored surface. If the painting is to be semitransparent, such as the leaves on a country-tin white band, trace very lightly, and do as much free-hand painting as possible.

Mother-of-Pearl Inlay

For centuries Oriental decoration made use of the inner layer of the shell of the nonedible oyster. This hard, silvery, brilliant shell layer that shows iridescent colors is called mother-of-pearl, and decorators of the Victorian period incorporated it into the designs on trays, boxes, tabletops, cabinets, and many other pieces. The mother-of-pearl became flowers, leaves, butterflies, insects, and even the windows of a castle or water in a moat. Crushed mother-of-pearl or small bits were used up by arranging them in patterns on the borders. The old shells were cut rather thick, so they looked white and were sometimes given a wash of transparent color and then overstrokes to represent petals, veins, etc. The mother-of-pearl that is available today is much thinner and when it is applied to a black background it is quite colorful but loses the pearly quality. It is sometimes necessary to paint an undercoat of white or silver on the articles before applying the pearl.

1. Give the article to be decorated one coat of sanding primer and sand smooth when it is dry.

2. Using a transfer paper, place the tracing of the pattern in position on the article and trace the outlines where the mother-of-pearl is to be applied.

3. Lay a piece of mother-of-pearl over the tracing and trace the design onto the pearl, using a pencil or ball-point pen.

4. Soak the pearl in a bowl of warm water until it can be cut easily with manicure scissors or similar small scissors. Keep it underwater while cutting and cut the sections a tiny bit larger than the tracing.

5. Dry the pearl, apply a coat of white shellac to the back and also to the area on the article where the pearl is to be placed. Allow the shellac to dry and repeat the shellacking process.

6. When the second application of shellac is tacky, press the pearl firmly onto the proper spot. Put a weight on it if possible. Elmer's Glue can also be used for the adhesive.

7. When thoroughly dry (about twenty-four hours) give the article three more coats of sanding primer, wiping it off the mother-of-pearl area between each coat.

8. Sand the primer coat smooth and apply as many coats of flat black as are needed to bring the background up to the level of the pearl. Clean off the pearl area each time. If the pearl is not perfectly clean, rub with wet-or-dry sandpaper and water and then with rottenstone and water. Wash and dry.

9. Apply any transparent washes that are needed and add the overstrokes when these are dry. Then proceed with the rest of the design.

Striping

My instructor, Mr. Crowell, once told about a student to whom he was teaching striping. After showing her the striping brush and demonstrating its use, the student went out to lunch and Mr. Crowell never saw her again! Some students quickly develop the art of striping; others develop the art of getting the teacher to do the striping for them. Each skill has virtue, for both indicate a real tenacity of purpose. Striping is really not that difficult. Confidence is the principal requirement, which, of course, means practice.

It is surprising to see the effect that striping can have on a design. An unstriped tray or chair is like an unframed picture. Chippendale or Gothic trays and other trays with elaborate designs were usually striped in gold, either leaf or powder. Trays or articles decorated with stencil or country-painting designs were almost always striped in a low-toned yellow, which was often used on the original pieces as an inexpensive substitute for gold. Other striping colors used less often, either alone or in combinations, were white, black, red, green, and a soft blue.

ABOVE: *Reproduction of stenciled button-back Hitchcock chair. Painted by Mrs. G. F.*   *Swenson.* BELOW: *Cornice board. Decorated by Flora Mears. [From* The Decorator*]*

1. Give the article to be striped a coat of varnish and when dry, rub with No. 0000 steel wool. This will make it easier for you to correct any mistakes.

2. Measure and draw guidelines as described under "White Bands," (page 98).

3. Mix the desired striping color on your palette and add enough varnish to make a soupy consistency.

4. Dip the striping brush in turpentine and wipe. Then lay it in the paint mixture and move it back and forth until all the hairs are covered. *Do not twist the brush.* When the brush is loaded, pull it across a clean part of your palette until a stripe of the desired width is obtained.

5. Hold the brush with thumb and forefinger and lay it on one of the guidelines, balancing the other fingers against the edge of the tray. Don't feel that you are painting the stripe. Just pull the brush toward you on the line; look where you are going

rather than where you have been. For painting a straight line, about two-thirds of the brush should be on the tray; but when going around a corner, raise the brush slightly so that only about one-third of the brush is doing the striping. Reload the brush when necessary, and lay it on the tray a little ahead of the stopping place.

6. If the stripe is gold, dust the varnished surface with talcum powder and use yellow enamel. When the enamel becomes tacky, rub it with bronze powder or lay gold leaf. Striping with bronze powder and varnish is not recommended except for patterns. The mixture does not flow evenly and the stripe usually looks dull and streaky.

7. When striping an octagonal tray, lay the brush with the point at one corner and pull it to within ½ to 1 inch of the next corner. Start with the point again at the second corner and draw to within the same distance of the third corner. Continue around the tray in this way. Then turn the tray around and place the brush with the point at the second corner headed toward the first, and fill in the gaps.

X

Finishing

SUPPLIES AND EQUIPMENT

Gloss Varnish   In recent years so many new ingredients have been used in the manu-
facture of paints and varnishes that it is difficult for the layman to know which
brands to choose or what results to expect. Pratt & Lambert's No. 61 Clear Gloss
Varnish, a favorite of many decorators, is still giving satisfactory results. Always
read the directions on the can to determine the proper solvent. Use the same varnish
throughout the decorating process on an article.

Colorless Varnish   Because most varnishes have a slightly yellow cast, a number of
coats will drastically change the color of a white or light-colored article. Eventually
a white tray could become bright yellow, a blue tray could become greenish, etc.
To prevent such discoloration, a colorless varnish is necessary. Pratt & Lambert's
No. 38, which comes in gloss and low luster; Hardcote No. 3071; and Rynalon
(tole finishes), which is alcohol-proof, are three colorless finishes.

Semigloss Varnish   Valspar Soft Gloss (Chippendale) is a very satisfactory finish
for articles which are not handrubbed. Many other companies produce nongloss varnishes; they usually come in three degrees of dullness. Unless you especially want a
very flat, dull finish, the glossiest product looks most like handrubbing.

Marine Spar Varnish   This varnish should be used for outdoor work since it has
waterproof qualities and is exceptionally durable.

Varnish Brush   A good varnish brush is a *must*. If properly cared for, it will last for several years, and is well worth the investment. Art & Sign's 1-inch ox-hair brush, Series No. 224, is very good. The same kind of brush used for painting backgrounds could also be used for varnishing if it is kept just for that purpose. To store the brush, fill a glass nursing bottle about half-full of turpentine. Cut off the rubber nipple at a point which will leave a hole large enough for the brush handle. Push the handle through, and place the cover on the bottle, allowing the brush to hang in the turpentine without touching the bottom. Screw the cover on tightly. (The last time I was in a drugstore buying a bottle for this purpose, the clerk tried to sell me one of the new plastic baby bottles; without thinking I asked, "Wouldn't turpentine dissolve the plastic?" Her face was a study!) If glass bottles eventually go off the market, an adequate, though not portable, substitute would be a tin can with a cardboard cover slit in the center to hold the brush handle.

Tack Rag   Tack rags can be bought at art supply stores. You can make one, however, by using a piece of fine cotton or linen, such as an old handkerchief. Dip the cloth in warm water and squeeze. Sprinkle it with turpentine and then pour on two or three teaspoonfuls of varnish. Twist and squeeze the cloth to work in the mixture. Store the tack rag in a closed jar. If it dries out, sprinkle with a little turpentine and water.

Finishing Powders   Rottenstone (see page 98) or pumice stone can be used. Pumice stone is a light gray powder used as an abrasive, so only the finest quality must be used. Dental powdered pumice (4F) is the most desirable. Both rottenstone and pumice can be found in paint or art supply stores.

Paraffin Oil and Crude Oil   Both paraffin oil and crude oil can be found in stores selling decorating supplies.

VARNISHING

A COMMON complaint among beginners is that they are unable to produce a perfectly smooth coat of varnish. Some books recommend precautions such as covering the floor of a north room with wet newspapers, and covering yourself from top to toe with lint-free material. The Chinese were said to have done their varnishing in boats some distance from shore, or in rooms partly flooded with water. For most people such elaborate preparations would be inconvenient, if not impossible, and they are not really necessary. But if you take no precautions, you cannot expect success. One student found her tray was sprinkled with various sorts of foreign matter, including a bug imbedded in one corner; she had set the tray on the attic windowsill to dry. With much diligent sanding and several additional coats of varnish, the finish turned out to be quite acceptable, but the remains of the bug were preserved between layers of varnish.

Somewhere between these extremes are reasonable precautions that should be taken. The first requirements are a clean, warm room, and dry weather.

1. Be sure that the article is clean and free from dust. A stenciled tray should be washed with mild soap and water and any spots of powder removed with a damp cloth and Lava soap. A painted design that includes no other techniques can be wiped *very lightly* with Energine to clean off tracing lines. Spots of paint can be removed with Energine or wet-or-dry sandpaper No. 600 dipped in water. A tack rag—which, as mentioned previously, can be made or bought—can be used to remove dust.

2. The varnish and the article should be at room temperature, at least 72 degrees. Do not shake the can of varnish. Shaking creates bubbles. If you are not using a new can, check the varnish to be sure it has not thickened or become lumpy. If it has, do not add a thinner. If it is thick due to cold, place the opened can in a pan of warm water for a few minutes. If there is any possibility of lumps in the varnish, strain it through a nylon stocking.

3. Use a good varnish brush—a 1-inch ox-hair is recommended—and if it has been hanging in turpentine, wipe it on newsprint or lint-free paper to remove the turpentine. If newspaper is used, the ink sometimes comes off on the brush.

Dip the brush into the varnish, lift it out without wiping it against the side of the container, and apply it to the article. This is called "flowing" on a coat of varnish.

4. Start with the area which is at an angle, such as the flange of a tray, where drips could form. It is not necessary to keep the brush going in the same direction, but work as quickly as possible. When the surface has been covered, break the bubbles by brushing *very lightly*. On a large tray or box, stroke from the two sides towards the center. Brush out any drips which have appeared. Dust particles and hairs can be flicked out with the corner of the brush. Varnish is self-leveling; but the minute it appears to be "setting up," it must not be touched. If varnishing a tray, wipe the underside of the edge and handholes to prevent drips.

5. Set the varnished article aside in a spot that is as dust-free as possible. A box cover with the sides cut for ventilation can be placed over it. A covered shelf is a good spot. Let it dry for at least twenty-four hours, or longer.

6. Apply another coat of varnish and allow to dry.

7. When the article is ready for the third coat of varnish and appears bumpy, sand it with wet-or-dry sandpaper No. 600 dipped in water.

8. After the article has had a minimum of five coats of varnish, set it aside to dry for *at least* forty-eight hours.

9. Now remove all bumps with wet-or-dry sandpaper No. 600 dipped in water. You can use a fair amount of pressure, although it is also possible to break through a coat of varnish. If this happens, Step 10 may solve the problem. Otherwise, the article will have to be revarnished and sanded.

10. When no bumps are visible, the gloss must be removed by rubbing with steel wool No. 0000. Rub with strokes going in the same direction when possible, and continue rubbing until the surface is completely dull. Some people prefer to use 4F powdered pumice and water for this step. When handrubbing a light-colored

Painted Windsor side chair. [*From* The Ornamented Chair]

*Windsor chair painted yellow, with freehand-
bronze decoration. From the Mrs. Arthur
Oldham collection.* [*From* The Ornamented
Chair]

article, substitute very fine garnet sandpaper for the wet-or-dry sandpaper, and 4F pumice for the steel wool and rottenstone.

Handrubbing

1. Sprinkle some rottenstone on the article and then pour on some crude oil, baby oil, or paraffin oil. Mix the rottenstone and oil, and rub all the surfaces thoroughly with a soft cloth or a piece of felt. Wipe off the mixture with a clean cloth and polish the piece with flannel. The cloths used for rubbing can be stored in a metal container and used many times.

2. If a glossier finish is desired, apply Butcher's bowling-alley wax, allow to dry, and polish with a soft cloth. There are also other finishing materials on the market, if you wish to experiment. Elizabeth Goodwin, a decorator whose husband was a violinmaker, uses the following mixture on semigloss varnish for the final hand (literally) rubbing: 2 parts baby oil; 2 parts raw linseed oil; 1 part ammonia and vinegar in equal amounts and rottenstone.

Other Finishes

Some pieces are too large or ornate to make a handrubbed finish practical. Furniture would be included in this group. For these pieces, the application of two coats of gloss varnish and one of semigloss varnish produces a satisfactory finish. Always stir the semigloss varnish so that the dulling agent is thoroughly mixed into the varnish. Be sure the surface that receives the semigloss varnish is absolutely smooth, as the final coat will not be rubbed.

The backs of trays can also be treated in this manner.

Antiquing

Five or six coats of varnish will have a softening effect on any decoration, but if further antiquing is desired and the background is black, add a little dark-oak varnish stain to the second or third coat of varnish.

For light backgrounds on either tin or wood, the following method of antiquing is effective. It is often used on furniture and is sometimes applied to give a streaky effect that becomes part of the decoration rather than being used to create the illusion of antiquity. Commercial kits put out by Glidden and the A. C. M. Company include the background paint as well as the antiquing materials, and are available at paint stores.

1. Be sure that the article has had a coat of varnish and has been carefully smoothed. On light-colored articles, use 4F pumice stone and water and, if necessary, very fine garnet sandpaper. The surface must be absolutely smooth, since any specks will pick up the glaze.

2. Check the directions on your can of varnish to see whether turpentine can be

used as a thinner—unless specifically prohibited, it can be used. Mix the varnish and turpentine in equal amounts; add some raw umber oil paint (the amount will depend on the desired tone), and mix thoroughly with a brush. If turpentine cannot be used, mix the umber with the unthinned varnish.

Vases with leaf, shield, and lyre designs; and pictorial urn. [Courtesy of the Cooper Union Museum, New York, New York]

Tray with painting and freehand bronzing on gold-leaf bands.

3. Paint the area to be antiqued with the mixture and quickly start rubbing with a soft, dry cloth. On small areas a No. 5 square-tipped quill could be used, and for larger areas such as a tabletop or bureau drawers, use an ox-hair background brush. Ordinarily, the glaze is almost rubbed off on the decoration, and the corners of the article are left darker. A soft, dry brush can also be used. If the glaze becomes sticky before you are satisfied with your efforts, wipe it off with varnish, let it dry, and the next time add a few drops of linseed oil to the mixture.

ALCOHOL-PROOF FINISH

SOME VARNISHES claim to be alcohol-proof or alcohol-resistant. Read the fine print on the can. If alcohol-proof or alcohol-resistant varnish is not available, others are quite good when rubbed down according to directions. Wipe any spots of liquor or water from the article as soon as possible, and rub the piece with finishing oil. If white spots appear later, rub with a little denatured alcohol or shellac thinner, and then immediately rub with the oil.

WEATHERPROOF FINISH

WHEN FINISHING something that is to be used outdoors, such as a decorated mailbox, sign, or patio table, use marine spar varnish.

XI

Reverse Painting on Glass

THE USE OF GLASS in decoration has a long history dating back to the early periods of Egyptian culture. By the tenth century, stained glass had become part of medieval architecture, and during succeeding centuries various methods of painting on glass were employed. Courting mirrors with decorated glass panels were among the exports when trade with China was flourishing, but some historians believe that this art was actually introduced by Jesuit missionaries and that much of the glass was imported from Europe.

In England, a method was devised to produce paintings on glass more quickly. These were called transfer paintings. An adhesive was applied to the back of the glass and an engraving, or mezzotint, which had been soaked in water, was pressed onto the glass. The paper backing was rubbed off with a wet sponge, leaving the engraving lines on the glass. Color was then applied, using the reverse-painting technique.

Portraits on glass became popular in America at the end of the eighteenth century. National heroes, statesmen, and many women were the subjects. Some were copies of famous American paintings, and others are thought to have been painted by itinerant artists. Artists in the Pennsylvania German area were especially productive.

The paintings of greatest interest to the student of decoration are those which are found on nineteenth-century clock and mirror glasses. They range from primitive paintings of buildings and trees to beautifully painted scenes with intricately etched gold-leaf borders, which are found in the more elegant mirror frames and clock cabinets. Other favorite subjects were portraits, figures, still lifes, boats, and even naval battles. Outlines and accent strokes were first painted in umber, although on some of the more formal scenes the building outlines look as if they had been done with a pen. The paintings often had stenciled or etched gold-leaf borders, and on other glasses entire designs were done in these techniques.

A collection of broken glass paintings is invaluable to anyone who wishes to study this technique in depth. Pieces are sometimes found in attics, and antique dealers and pickers occasionally discover them. They cannot be mended, and they are of no value except as sources of designs for reproduction. Besides providing material from which to work, glass fragments—better than could any list of directions—illustrate the methods that were used. Preserve the pieces by taping them on a piece of glass and covering them with another glass.

SUPPLIES AND EQUIPMENT

Japan Drier   This is a liquid which is sometimes added to paints or varnishes to speed drying. It contains petroleum distillate and lead, so it is *poisonous*. It should be used in a well-ventilated room, and kept out of the reach of children.

Gelatin Capsules   These capsules can be purchased at a drugstore. They are the clear, empty capsules that are used for holding vitamins or drugs.

Ruling Pen   This is a pen with two long prongs which can be adjusted to produce lines of various widths. As long as the outside of each prong is clean, there is no danger of a blob of ink forming. Compasses with ruling pens are helpful for drawing circles in ink. These are architects' supplies and can be purchased at art supply stores.

Templates and French Curves   Templates are described in Chapter III. French curves are usually made of plastic and look like a combination of various types of scrolls. The edges can be used as guides for drawing curves of different sizes and degrees.

STENCILING ON GLASS

ON CLOCK and mirror glasses stenciling was used for the entire design or it was combined with gold leaf and/or painting. In a combination of techniques, stenciling was generally used in the border design.

1. Trace the outlines of the entire design in ink on tracing paper. If it is a one-piece stencil, and the architects' linen is thin enough, the design can be traced directly onto the linen. If it is a composite stencil, the linen can be laid over the tracing and the single units traced, leaving an inch of linen around each unit.

2. Cut out the stencil or stencils as described in Chapter III.

3. If possible, use an old piece of glass, and have it cut to the proper size. Clean it thoroughly with a moist cloth and cleansing powder, Lava soap, or whiting powder. Rinse with clear water and dry.

4. Reverse the tracing, tape it to a piece of cardboard, and position the glass over the tracing. Tape the top of the glass to the cardboard, letting the masking tape cover only the $\frac{1}{16}$ of an inch which will be covered by the frame rabbet. Attach a piece of folded tape to the middle of the bottom of the glass so that you can move the glass without touching it.

5. Flow a thin coat of varnish over the entire glass with an ox-hair varnish brush; be especially careful to keep it dust-free. Spray varnish can be used, but it must be sprayed in both directions to assure an even coat. It is helpful to varnish another small piece of glass to use for testing. Place both pieces of glass under a box cover to protect them from dust while drying.

6. Test the tack periodically by pressing a piece of architects' linen on the test glass or on the edge of the larger glass. If the tack is right—the same as for stenciling on tin or wood—lay the first stencil unit on the glass, using the tracing as a guide. If the design is a composite stencil, the first unit should be the object in the foreground which shows completely.

7. Slip a piece of black paper between the glass and the tracing, and apply the bronze powder as described in Chapter III. After stenciling the first unit, remove the black paper and the tracing will act as a guide for placement of the next stencil unit. Stenciling on glass should be done with special care because corrections and repairs are not easy to make. If a spot is rubbed off, taking the varnish with it, this spot will show from the front even if it is revarnished.

Lace-edge tray. [*Courtesy of the* Cooper Union Museum, New York, New York]

8. When the glass is dry—allow at least twenty-four hours—wash it with mild soap and water, and dry. If there are any spots which need to be removed, try rubbing on the test glass with a moist cloth and Lava soap, or with a pencil eraser, to see if you can take off the powder without rubbing through the varnish. If you are successful with the test glass, repair the main glass; then give the glass another coat of varnish.

9. When the varnish is dry, paint in the colors. Opaque colors backing up stencil units are often found on borders and should be painted to the edge of the stencil. Although the bronze powder may be solid at the edge, it is not always opaque enough to disguise the cut-off line.

10. After the glass has dried for a few days, apply the background paint. Background colors for stencils were usually black, black asphaltum, or a dark color. White or light tints were sometimes used when the stencil units were backed up with opaque color. For a black background use flat or enamel paint. Asphaltum was often used in place of black because it produced a much warmer tone. It can be thinned with a little varnish if necessary. Colors can be mixed by adding tube colors to prepared paints (chrome yellow added to black makes a nice olive green) or to striping white in japan. A mixture of only tube oil colors does not produce the proper consistency for background paint. Depending on the size of the area, use a large square-tipped quill, a bright's red sable, or an ox-hair stroke brush for applying the paint.

GOLD LEAF ON GLASS

IN THE past, gold leaf was used alone or in combination with other techniques on mirror and clock glasses, as well as on other decorative glass panels. There are endless possibilities for present-day use. Anyone with imagination can adapt old designs or create new ones for the decoration of glass ashtrays, hot pads, box tops, panels for mirror frames, or glass tops for coffee tables and nests of tables. An artist friend, who learned how to apply gold leaf to glass, decorated a large glass coffee table with a gold-leaf tiger. Using gold leaf on glass is probably one of the most versatile techniques.

PREPARING THE GLASS

1. Trace the design in ink on tracing paper and cut the paper to exactly the size of the glass.

2. Clean the glass by wiping carefully with a moist cloth and cleansing powder, Lava soap, or whiting powder; then dry with a paper towel. Position the glass over the reversed tracing and tape it to the corners of the tracing.

3. Black lines on gold leaf that are too wide to be produced by etching must be painted and allowed to dry before the leaf is laid. India ink or any water-soluble paint cannot be used because it would disappear when the gelatin size is applied.

Flat-black paint with a little turpentine or japan drier makes the best paint. The narrow black bands that separate the borders from the center designs should be made with a ruling pen and ruler—or with a striping brush, if you have a steady hand. Cross the lines at the corners and either wipe off the extensions while the paint is wet, or let them dry and then scrape them off with an X-acto knife. A small, pointed red-sable brush can be used for strokes or lines of varied widths.

APPLYING THE GOLD LEAF

1. The gelatin size that causes the leaf to adhere to the glass can be made with either a gelatin capsule or powdered gelatin; I prefer the capsule. Add the small half of a No. oo gelatin capsule to about 1 cup of distilled water and bring to a boil. Pour the mixture into a glass jar. Pour through a nylon stocking if the gelatin seems lumpy. Use the size while it is hot.

When using powdered gelatin, add a little cold water to ⅛ teaspoon of gelatin. Let the mixture sit until it is completely dissolved. Add ¾ cup of boiling water, strain, and use hot. The gelatin solution becomes more concentrated as it is used, so it is wise to mix a new jarful occasionally, rather than to continue dipping into the first mixture until it is down to the last drop. A strong concentration of gelatin will cause the gold leaf to look cloudy.

2. Be sure to use glass gold leaf (unmounted) since this has the fewest imperfections. The best way to apply the gold leaf is by the method described in Steps 2 and 3 under "Applying Gold Leaf to Irregular Surfaces" in Chapter V. (See also *Gilder's Cushion* under "Supplies and Equipment," page 57.) Prop the glass with the tracing behind it on edge at a slight angle on a table easel or on the table with a support. Arrange a few layers of paper tissues under the edge to absorb the excess size. Using a large, soft, camel-hair brush, flood the portion of the glass to be gilded with the hot size. Pass the gilder's tip across your cheek and lay the tip over one edge of the sheet of gold leaf. Pick it up carefully and flip it onto the glass in the proper place. Apply as many pieces as are needed to cover the area, allowing the pieces to overlap. Flow on more size as you continue the process.

3. There is another method of applying the gold leaf. It is frowned on by purists but is much easier, especially for beginners, and it involves the use of wax paper to pick up the gold leaf. If possible, use luncheon wax paper in sheets rather than the rolls because the sheets are thinner and have less wax.

Open a book of gold leaf part way, slip a piece of wax paper over a sheet, and close the book. Rub the cover gently, and not as firmly as you would for gold leaf on tacky size (Chapter V). It is not necessary for the leaf to adhere completely to the paper, because the whole sheet must leave the paper. It is possible to cut the mounted leaf with scissors if smaller pieces are needed. Leave the glass lying flat on the table and flood the area to be worked with size. (I have used both hot and cold size with this method with no difference in the results.) Hold the mounted gold leaf with both hands, leaf side down, about ½ inch from the glass in the proper spot and drop it.

Gallery tray with portrait medallion. [*Courtesy of the* Cooper Union Museum, New York, New York]

The size acts like a magnet to the gold leaf so try to drop the wax paper and leaf so that the entire sheet hits the glass at the same time. After a second or two lift a corner of the wax paper and peel it off, leaving the leaf on the glass. Continue in the same way, overlapping the sheets. Don't worry if the leaf is somewhat wrinkled; the excess will rub off after it is dry. Cracks can be patched but it is best to apply a second layer of gold leaf to repair any holidays.

4. When the entire area is covered (by whichever method used), set the glass at an angle on a table easel or supported from the back so that the excess size can run off the glass. If placed in the sun or under a lamp, the glass will dry more quickly. When it is dry, the gold leaf will show a slight burnish.

5. When the gold leaf is thoroughly dry (wait for several hours if it has not been exposed to extra warmth), brush off the excess gold with absorbent cotton and rub very gently to increase the burnish.

6. Heat some water to the boiling point. Hold the glass over the heating unit briefly to warm it; then hold it at an angle over the sink and pour the boiling water over the gold leaf. This gives it more of a burnish. When this is dry, rub again gently with absorbent cotton and apply another layer of gold leaf by repeating Steps 2 or 3 through 6.

117]

ETCHING THE GOLD LEAF

1. After burnishing the second layer of leaf, the design must be traced onto the gold. Tape the tracing over the glass (reversed, as it was under the glass) and slip a piece of graphite paper between the tracing and the glass. With a stylus or hard pencil trace the outlines of the gold units and if there is any etching, indicate the general placement. It is not a good idea to trace the etching lines because this kind of shading is more effective when done freehand.

2. Remove the tracing. If the traced lines do not show clearly on the gold, dust a thin film of lithopone powder over the lines with a soft brush. This should make them easier to see; but if you still have difficulty, place a light bulb in a box that has a piece of frosted glass laid over its top. Lay the gilded glass on the frosted glass, gold side up; the light from the bulb should make the lines discernible and ready for etching.

3. If the tracing lines are visible without working over a light, lay the glass over a piece of black paper so that the lines etched through the gold will appear black. A number of different tools can be used for etching: the triple etcher used for gold leaf on tin or wood, an X-acto knife, a penpoint, a stylus, a sharpened bamboo stick, or even a toothpick, depending on the width and character of the lines. Experiment with several tools to find out what each will do. Templates or French curves can be used to true up circles, ovals, and curves, but they must be laid on some soft material so that the gold leaf will not be scratched.

4. Outline all the units with single lines. Etching lines that represent shading are done with either a single or triple etcher. It is easy to tell which tool has been used because the lines made with the single etcher will not be so uniform. Don't be afraid to etch heavily. You may feel that you are overetching, but for some reason the lines never appear as heavy on the right side of the glass as they do on the reverse. A gold-leaf band should have a single line on either side. Use a bridge to steady the etching tool.

BACKING UP THE DESIGN

1. When the etching is completed to your satisfaction, the design must be backed up with a dark paint so that the lines will contrast with the gold on the front side of the glass. This can be done with black enamel, black seal, or black asphaltum. The latter seems to have been used for many of the old glasses. Add 6 drops of japan drier to 1 teaspoon of asphaltum and paint the outlined gold units solidly, both those that are etched and those that are not. Use enough paint to hold the gold when the excess is rubbed off, but not so much that it will "creep" at the edges.

2. For greater protection give the fine lines or strokes a second application of paint when the first is dry. Another method of increasing the resistance of the paint is to rub litharge into the paint with a soft brush while it is still tacky. This yellow powder is a lead compound and, therefore, *poisonous*. It should be used carefully and kept away from the skin or mouth.

3. When the paint is thoroughly dry (at least forty-eight hours), lay the glass over black paper and rub off all the gold which has not been backed up with paint. Use absorbent cotton that has been moistened with water and dipped in whiting powder. Saliva works well, too! Be very careful when working over fine lines because if any of the painted gold is rubbed off, the whole process—laying the leaf, etching, and painting—must be repeated. For hard-to-remove specks near the units, an X-acto knife is helpful. After all the excess gold has been removed from the glass, it is ready for the background paint.

PAINTING ON GLASS

IN THIS type of decoration the paint is applied to the back of the glass and the order of application is the reverse of that used on tin and wood. Instead of preparing a background and then painting the base coats, shadows and highlights, and finally the overstrokes, the accent strokes and outlines are painted first, followed by the shadows and highlights, the main areas of color, and finally the background. The paint used on many of the old glasses was an opaque watercolor and the brush work seems to have been done fairly quickly and with authority. Most decorators, however, use oil paint to make reproductions of these old glasses. It is a more familiar medium, for it is used in the other painting techniques covered in preceding chapters and the effect when viewed from the right side is much the same.

If the painting you are copying has a stenciled or gold-leaf border, this must be done first (gold leaf and then stenciling if they are combined) and the background color must be applied before the center design is painted. This order of procedure allows more freedom when painting the areas next to the border. The color can overlap the border without showing through the background paint.

If you are reproducing an authentic old mirror or clock glass, try to find a piece of old glass. It is much thinner than the kind presently available and has some imperfections; but the effect of the finished painting will be more like an original.

1. Clean the glass thoroughly, using a damp cloth and Lava soap, Babo, or whiting powder.

2. Make a tracing of the design in ink on tracing paper, reverse it, and place it under the glass. Both tracing and glass can be taped to a piece of cardboard.

3. If there is a stenciled or gold-leaf border, do this first, following the directions given earlier in this chapter under "Stenciling on Glass" and "Gold Leaf on Glass." Sometimes there are burnt-umber lines and strokes, or stippling in a combination of colors, surrounding the gold-leaf or stenciled units. These must be painted before the background color is applied. For the lines and strokes use a scroller and small watercolor brush. The stippling can be done with a piece of sponge or a stencil brush held in a perpendicular position. This is like a dry-brush technique in which no vehicle is added to the paint and the color is broken so that the background and color spots are somewhat evenly distributed.

4. When the design is dry, paint the background on the border, following the directions in Step 10 under "Stenciling on Glass." When the background paint is dry,

the tracing of the center design can be cut from the border and taped to the front of the glass.

5. If there are buildings in the design which appear to be outlined with pen lines, the glass should be treated so that the ink will flow evenly from the pen. Either give the glass a thin coat of varnish and set it under a box to dry, or treat it with cleaning fluid and powder, as explained under "Tinsel Painting" page 122. The lines can be drawn with a tracing or a crow-quill pen and brown or black drawing ink. Use either a felt-backed ruler or a bridge as a guide. If it seems difficult to get sharp corners, cross the converging lines and clean off the extensions with an X-acto knife. If the glass has been varnished, the knife might cut through; so it would be wise to wipe the excess off before it has dried, or wipe it carefully with a moist cloth.

6. If the outlines have been painted with a brush and burnt umber, the glass does not have to be treated. Mix the paint with a little varnish and if this does not produce a deep enough tone, mix the umber with a little flat black and less varnish. Use a scroller for fine lines and either a small square-tipped quill or a pointed red-sable brush for the strokes. Paint all lines and accent strokes which appear in colors other than umber. Mistakes should be wiped off with cleaning fluid, for turpentine will leave a film on the glass.

7. When this layer of paint is dry (twenty-four to forty-eight hours), look at the design for areas of color which overlap other colors but which are not overlaid with any strokes except the ones in the first painting. Tree trunks, rocks, foreground foliage, shadows on buildings, fruit, and clothing might come under this category. When two colors are blended in one area, mix up each color and add a very small amount of varnish. Using either a No. 3 square-tipped quill or a bright's red-sable brush No. 8, paint each mixture where it appears. Blend the colors at once with the bright's brush. Check on the front of the glass, and if the line between the colors is still evident, rub it with your finger to push the colors together; then brush lightly along the blended area.

8. Let this layer dry thoroughly. Next paint another group of objects which appear to be behind the areas just painted. These should not touch each other, however. Buildings, water, grass, distant hills, and drapery might be painted in this step. The drapery borders occasionally show designs that have been cut through the paint. To get this effect, paint the entire border; then, while the paint is still wet, draw the design through the paint with a toothpick or similar tool. When the back-up paint is applied, the design will appear in that color. This operation will have to be done freehand since you will not be able to see tracing lines through the border paint; but the designs usually consist of a series of simple lines and squiggles that should not be difficult to duplicate.

9. Continue painting succeeding layers, allowing plenty of drying time between each, until every part of the design has been painted except the sky (if it is a scene) or the background color. If the background is one color, mix the desired color and paint it on with a No. 5 square-tipped quill, a No. 8 bright's red sable, or an ox-hair stroke brush. Prepared paints can be used for this background. If a light shade is

needed, use flat white and add tube oil color to produce the proper tint. Skies often change from blue to yellow to pink, and other background colors sometimes shade from a light to a dark tone. Apply these colors and blend them as directed in Step 7.

10. Painting clouds is fun. Pick up some white oil paint on the index finger and rub it into the wet sky with a rotary motion. It takes quite a bit of white to push through the other colors. Hold the glass on edge, watching it from the front and working on the back. As you rub more gently and in smaller circles the cloud seems to fade off into the distance.

REPAIRING ORIGINAL GLASSES

A PAINTED glass should be repaired rather than reproduced if only a small portion of the paint has flaked off.

1. Pick off all the paint which has already lifted from the glass and give the entire painting a coat of spray varnish. This protective coat must be sprayed on because a brush would loosen particles of paint which could otherwise be saved.

2. If there are any strokes or lines missing, these must be painted and allowed to dry before being backed up by the color.

3. Mix a color which matches as closely as possible the color surrounding the area to be patched. (See Chapter II on color.)

4. Load a brush with a little varnish and a bit of the paint mixture, and paint a stroke or two on the edge of another piece of glass which has been varnished.

5. When this is dry, hold the front of the test glass against the front of the original to see if there is any difference in value or intensity between the two colors. Oil colors tend to darken when they are dry, so a small amount of white may have to be added to the mixture. Your paint mixture should stay soft for several hours but if you will not be using it for a longer period, cover it with Saran Wrap or put it in a small container and fill with water to cover the paint.

6. Load a square-tipped quill with the corrected paint mixture and paint over the open area. If you are unsure about the color, paint a stroke on the test glass again and repeat Step 5 until you are satisfied with the match. If the spots to be patched are quite small, the paint can be picked up on the index finger and patted onto the openings.

Repairing gold leaf and stenciled designs is not quite as simple. It would be wise to consult an expert before doing anything to damaged areas. These glasses are often more valuable when left untouched except for a protective coat of spray varnish. The etching on some of the more elegant gold-leaf borders is so fine that only an experienced decorator should reproduce it. On the other hand some gold-leaf designs which cover the entire glass are etched very crudely. They are generally scenes with buildings and trees, and reflect the charm of nineteenth-century folk art.

1. If a simple gold-leaf unit needs repair, scrape off the entire unit, clean the exposed glass, and follow the directions given under "Gold Leaf on Glass." If the

leaf does not match the original and the difference is quite obvious, all similar units will have to be replaced.

2. When the back-up paint on the etched gold leaf has dried, mix the background color and apply it as directed in Step 9 under "Painting on Glass."

TINSEL PAINTING

THIS TYPE of glass decoration—sometimes called Pearl, or Oriental, painting—was popular in the mid-nineteenth century, but is not often included in information about reverse glass-painting. Examples are not plentiful and some are disappointingly crude. The designs, which were most often flowers and birds, were executed in transparent colors with a black or white background painted around the details. The paintings were backed up with crumpled tin foil which gave the transparent portions a jewel-like appearance.

According to Marian Cooney, a decorator who is an expert in tinsel painting, mica was often used to achieve the crystallized or sparkly effect. This mineral can be divided into thin, transparent sheets, pulled apart in small, thin pieces, and applied to the wet medium with tweezers. She also tells us that the lead or tin foil used to back up the paintings was obtained from tea packages. Glass box tops and tabletops, as well as framed pictures, were treated in this manner; but aside from these, modern decorators haven't come up with many variations. Because of the lack of old designs, flower prints can be adapted very successfully.

1. Make a complete tracing of the design on tracing paper, using either a pencil or a crow-quill pen with colored drawing ink.

2. Clean the glass thoroughly with a moist cloth and Babo, Lava soap, or whiting powder.

3. The next step is preparing the glass to receive ink outlines. Without special treatment it is difficult to produce an even line on glass with pen and ink. There are several methods which can be used to make such drawing easier. The glass can be sprayed with varnish and allowed to dry—but it will be impossible to scrape off any unwanted lines without cutting through the varnish. Or flow on or blow with a fixative blower a coat of alcohol or shellac thinner with about 2 drops of shellac to 1 tablespoon of thinner. Perhaps the most satisfactory method is rubbing Energine or cleaning fluid on the glass, sprinkling it with talcum powder, and rubbing again with the same cloth from which much of the fluid has evaporated. This removes most of the powder.

4. Place the glass, treated side up, over the reversed tracing and tape the two together at the upper corners.

5. With a tracing pen or crow-quill pen, and black ink, trace all the lines except the groups of fine lines which represent shadows and any curlycues, tendrils, or fine stems. The shadow lines should be done freehand, following the placement and general direction in the tracing. Try using the back of the penpoint for very fine

lines. If the background of the tinsel picture is white and there are black curlycues and tendrils, they can be traced at this time. On black backgrounds or when these fine lines appear in color, another method, described in Step 9, is used. Slip a piece of white paper between the tracing and glass occasionally to check on the width of the pen lines.

6. When the glass tracing is completed, check for blobs, line extensions, and other mistakes. Scrape these off with an X-acto knife and make any other necessary corrections.

7. The background color should be painted next. This is the tedious part; but if it is done first, the transparent colors used for the design can be applied with more freedom. If the transparent colors should run over the ink outline onto the background, the color would not show through. Use a semigloss or enamel paint in black or white. The white can be slightly tinted with oil color, but be careful to add only a very small amount. The paint appears much brighter after it has been applied.

8. With a pointed red-sable brush, paint the background around the outlined units in the center of the design, unless no background shows in this area. Don't worry if the paint seems streaky and lumpy. This is one time when it is not necessary for the brush strokes to flow together evenly into an absolutely smooth surface. When the glass is viewed from the front, the paint appears miraculously smooth, and if any spots are too thin they can be repainted when the first coat is dry. After finishing the small areas between the different units in the design, the larger areas around the outside edges can be painted with a large square-tipped quill or an ox-hair stroke brush, the size depending on the size of the picture.

9. While the background paint is still wet, lay the tracing beside the glass, and using a toothpick or the pointed end of a brush handle, draw all curlycues, tendrils, and fine stems (which have not already been done in ink) into the wet paint. These must be drawn freehand, but you can judge the position and form by glancing at the tracing. Use a bridge (see Figure 7) across the glass to support your hand and keep it away from the wet paint.

10. When the background paint is dry, use an X-acto knife to scrape off any spots which have gone over the outline onto the design.

11. The design is now painted with transparent colors mixed with varnish. If there are any white flowers, use titanium-white oil color in place of striping white in japan, since japan colors are too opaque for this type of painting. First paint any accents, such as dots or lines, that have hard edges which do not blend into the main color.

12. Let these accent strokes dry; then, using a square-tipped quill, lay on the light shade of one of the transparent colors wherever it appears. Test the color on white paper or another piece of glass backed up with crumpled aluminum foil. It is sometimes hard to judge the proper value or intensity of the color until you see it over the foil. Next paint in the shadow areas of these units and blend into the light shade by spreading the brush hairs and stroking lightly. If the light shade of paint has set up, let it dry completely; then paint the shadows and blend with clear varnish.

Use deep shadow colors where the base of a leaf meets the outer edge of the flower so that it will appear to be behind the flower.

13. If there is a white flower in the design, first paint the entire flower or petal (if they are separated) with a square-tipped quill and a mixture of titanium white and varnish. Use a mixture thin enough to make the flower look pearly when backed up with foil. Mix the shadow color (raw umber with a little Prussian blue is a good combination) and paint some strokes from the center of the flower out. Try to curve the strokes so they will follow the contour of the petal. Clean the brush, moisten with varnish, and press the tip to flatten and widen it. Stroke from the white area down into the deep-shadow tone until the two are blended. After each stroke, wipe off the tip of the brush (I use my fingers) to prevent the deeper color you pick up each time from showing on the white in the next stroke.

14. When the paint is dry fit the picture into a frame. Old walnut frames with gold liners can be used for pictures with white backgrounds, and gold frames are effective with either black or white backgrounds. Crumple a piece of aluminum foil and lay it over the picture. Either the dull or the shiny side can be down but the former seems to make the design hold together better. Cover with a piece of cardboard and tack in place.

XII

Problems and Solutions

I N USING the various techniques described in the preceding chapters, you may have run into problems not discussed in the text. For this reason, solutions for some of the more common problems are discussed chapter-by-chapter in the following pages.

COUNTRY PAINTING (CHAPTER I)

Brush strokes are spread on the edges.
It could be that your mixture of paint and varnish is too thin; but, more likely, you did not dress the brush sufficiently.

Tails of the brush strokes are thick.
If the brush is properly loaded, the position at the beginning of the strokes may not have been correct—that is, the knife edge may not have been pointed toward you. Or you may not have raised the brush enough as you finished the stroke with the knife edge.

Base coats do not cover the black background.
If you are using an oil paint, it may not be very opaque. If such is the case, paint two layers, letting the first dry thoroughly. Be careful not to let the edges build up. If you are using japan paint, it should cover in one layer. Use a little more paint, and when brushing across your strokes, be sure that you press out the tip of the

square-tipped quill to make it at least ⅜ inch wide. Unless the brush is wide and flat, it will pick up the paint rather than smooth it out.

Edges of base coats are fuzzy.
If the paint is still wet, just moisten a red-sable bright's or a pointed brush with turpentine, and draw it with some pressure along the outer edge of the painting. Clean the brush and repeat if necessary. *Do not use this method of cleanup if the base coat is to receive bronze powder or leaf.*

COLOR AND ADDITIONAL PAINTING TECHNIQUES (CHAPTER II)

Floated color is blotchy.
If the floated color hasn't dried thoroughly, remove it with varnish and redo, using a drop or two of linseed oil in the varnish to slow the drying. Be sure to flatten and widen the quill as was done for blending the base coats.

Floated color shows on black background.
Some so-called transparent colors are not completely transparent. Actually, in some of the old paintings the floated color was not very transparent; but if you are not a purist, moisten a square-tipped quill with turpentine and wipe up the paint on the background while the paint is still wet.

Lines that should be long and fine are thick and thin.
A new scroller sometimes needs "breaking in," so don't become discouraged. Be sure that the paint mixture is thin enough to flow easily and that the brush is held almost perpendicular. Always moisten the brush with oil and point the tip before storing. If this does not help, try using an Art & Sign pointed quill, Series 480, No. 1, instead of the scroller.

STENCILING (CHAPTER III)

Powder does not blend well and looks grainy.
Make sure that you are using a *lining* powder. Coarse bronze powders are useful only on solid areas.

Bronze powder does not blend and the velvet sticks.
The varnish is probably too wet (not the proper tack).

The velvet moves easily, but the powder looks dark and shiny.
The varnish has become too dry. Allow it to dry thoroughly, rub off the stencil with Lava soap, revarnish, and restencil. If you are aware that the varnish is too dry before you start stenciling, wipe a cloth moistened with turpentine over the surface

and apply the stencil. The turpentine softens the varnish, producing a slight tack. This would not be practical for a large area or a stencil with a great deal of shading.

Edges of the stencil units look blurred.
You may be using a coarse bronze powder, or the edges of the linen may not be properly pressed down onto the varnished surface, thus allowing the powder to spray underneath. Be sure that the stencil has been cleaned thoroughly on both sides. Some of the sprayed powder may disappear when the pattern is washed with soap and water before varnishing, but if the units still look blurred, remove them with a damp cloth and Lava soap. When dry, revarnish the entire design, and restencil the missing units. Several coats of varnish will correct any difference in tone.

Stencil sticks to the varnish.
Obviously, the varnish is too wet. If the stencil has left a mark when you remove it, wait a while and the mark may disappear. If not, allow the varnish to dry thoroughly (twenty-four hours), sand with wet-or-dry sandpaper No. 600 with water, and re-varnish.

The paint does not rub into the velvet.
If you are using cotton velvet, it may have been treated with Scotchgard. To remove it, wash in a washing machine with Downy or a similar softener.

There is a spot of paint on the velvet.
As mentioned in the directions, there is no reliable remedy for this problem. Spot another piece of velvet and try out some spray-on spot removers. I have been fairly successful in removing light spotting with Afta, a product of Afta Solvents Corporation.

FREEHAND BRONZE (CHAPTER IV)

Black enamel is too thick.
If you wish to use the paint right away, add a little varnish to thin it out. If the paint has become thick and lumpy in the can, strain it through a nylon stocking, add a little turpentine, and store it in a baby-food jar or covered container.

Black seal does not cover the background.
Occasionally the black seal seems too thin to produce a solid-black base coat. You could ask for a replacement at the store where you bought it; but if this is inconvenient, add some black oil paint or leave the can open for a few days so that it will thicken.

Cloudiness shows on black background.
If some cloudiness still remains around bronzed units after washing and erasing, it is

possible to paint around the units with the background paint. This is a last-resort measure, however, and the edge of the new paint must be rubbed onto the background (I use my finger) so that no line will show.

GOLD LEAF (CHAPTER V)

Small repairs are needed after size has dried.
To produce quality results, repairs on gold-leaf units should be made before the size has dried. Under some circumstances, however—when there are pinhole-size holidays covered with etching or shading, for example—the area can be brushed with a tiny bit of white shellac and the gold leaf pressed on very shortly afterwards. The leaf will be brighter than the rest of the unit so it will show up unless it is in a very inconspicuous spot or covered later.

Gold leaf looks dull and coarse.
The size was probably too wet when it was laid. For best results, wipe off the unit with turpentine or Energine, let dry, and powder before repainting.

A sheet of gold leaf is folded in the book.
If a corner of the leaf has turned back as the book was being opened, it can be flattened out by blowing under the folded edge *very gently*. If the leaf has been folded for some time, remove the leaf on wax paper as previously directed. When it is applied, only the first layer of leaf will adhere to the size, leaving the other layer for use on the next area.

Gold leaf sticks to the background.
The varnished background may not have dried enough before you applied the leaf; or you probably failed to apply a thin film of talcum powder before painting the design. The thin layer of talcum powder should be used on all backgrounds except those on which *flat* paint is used. Even commercial backgrounds occasionally pick up bits of gold leaf. If only a small amount of gold has adhered to the background, it can be removed with Energine, powdered pumice, or an X-acto knife, depending on the location.

Etching does not give an effect of form.
Does the etching stroke start where the deepest shadow is indicated, and taper off where the light begins? Do the etching lines follow the proper curve? Study the illustrations of modeling in Chapter VI.

CHIPPENDALE PAINTING (CHAPTER VI)

Flowers look flat and stiff.
Add more shadows and highlights, as indicated in the section on modeling.

Lace-edge tray with handles. [Courtesy of the
Cooper Union Museum, New York, New
York]

Color is too bright.
If the paint has not dried, it can be rubbed off with varnish and the area can be repainted. If the paint is dry, float a wash or glaze of transparent color over the whole
unit. A thin wash of raw umber and varnish over blues and greens, and burnt umber
and varnish over reds and yellows will cut the intensity.

Flowers do not look filmy.
Have you built up the layers of paint *gradually* from transparent to opaque? Make
sure that an edge of the preceding, more transparent layer is visible when painting
each succeeding layer of petals. This creates a softening effect around the edge of
the flower. Keep the contrast between values definite; that is, make the dark areas
dark and the light ones light. When painting overlapping petals, let the sharp light
edge of the petal blend down gradually to a deeper value before meeting the sharp
light edge of the overlapping petal or it will not appear as another petal.

LACE-EDGE PAINTING (CHAPTER VII)

The problems presented by lace-edge painting are similar to those encountered in
the preceding chapter, since the subject matter is much the same. The only difference
is in the substitution of the wax medium for varnish. You will be able to use this new
medium effectively if you follow directions carefully and practice.

PREPARATION OF TIN AND WOOD (CHAPTER VIII)

Background paint is ridgy.
This often happens in a beginner's first effort. Chances are that the priming coats are ridgy rather than (or in addition to) the background paint. No matter how much sanding is done or how smooth the background feels, the ridges generally show up in succeeding layers of paint or varnish. It is therefore necessary to strip the article and start again, using an ox-hair brush and thinner paint. Some spray-can paints are useful if the surface is smooth and the paint is compatible with succeeding layers of paint and varnish.

Red sanding primer dries too fast to paint a smooth coat.
Add a little Penetrol to the primer. This is an additive which makes paints easier to apply. If the paint still dries too fast, add a little more Penetrol.

Primer or paints don't dry.
If the paint doesn't dry, or if it looks dry but a slight scratch with the fingernail lifts it from the surface, something is wrong. There could be a number of reasons for this. Painting on a damp day or water in the paintbrush might hold up the drying process; in these instances, a little more waiting time will take care of the problem. If the paint is old or not thoroughly stirred, there could be too much oil. There might be oil or some other material under the paint which had not been cleaned off. The safest thing to do would be to strip the article, wipe it with cider vinegar, and repaint.

Flat black dries gray.
Certain brands of flat black dry a gray color but turn black when they are varnished.

APPLYING THE DECORATION (CHAPTER IX)

Graphite tracing lines are too heavy.
When tracing on a light-colored or white background, a fresh piece of graphite paper will leave lines so heavy that they show through the paint. Either rub or brush powdered pumice (4F) lightly over the tracing until the lines are barely visible.

Striping is thick and thin.
If you are using a sword striper which has been loaded correctly, you may be exerting uneven pressure on it. If you are using a striping quill, the mixture may not be sufficiently fluid or the brush may not have been dressed enough on the palette to distribute the mixture evenly throughout the bristles. Or perhaps you are trying to "paint" with the brush rather than pulling it along the surface.

The stripe spreads.
The mixture is too thin. Add more paint.

FINISHING (CHAPTER X)

Varnish doesn't dry.
This is a little more serious than nondrying paint, since the varnish cannot be removed without damaging the decoration. It should not happen if the surface has been thoroughly cleaned (vinegar cuts any greasy film left by fingerprints, etc.), if the varnish is not old, and if the brush which has been suspended in turpentine has been wiped so that no turpentine remains on it. If the varnish has not dried within a reasonable time, place it in a warm oven or in a stream of warm air from a hair dryer. As a last resort, if the only alternative is to strip and repaint the article, give it a coat of white shellac and continue with the varnish coats. The shellac itself will dry and isolate the tacky varnish. This advice is technically unsound as, theoretically, a fast-drying medium applied over a slow-drying medium will eventually produce crackle. Therefore, it is mentioned as something to do at your own risk, although I have done this in one or two emergencies without disastrous results. Old trays are often badly crackled, and I have had trays crackle when all precautions were followed; so when dealing with paints and varnishes, the reason for some results will always remain a mystery.

Spots show on background under first coat of varnish.
If some spots of paint or powder still show when the first coat of varnish is applied, rub them while the varnish is wet, with wet-or-dry sandpaper No. 500 used dry, and then stroke lightly with the varnish brush.

An excessive amount of dust is in the varnish coat.
If the situation doesn't appear hopeless, sprinkle some powdered pumice (4F) on the article, add a little water, and sand with wet-or-dry sandpaper No. 600 until all the bumps have disappeared.

One layer of varnish has rubbed through.
If this happens on the last coat of varnish, rub the article thoroughly with No. 0000 steel wool and finish with rottenstone and rubbing oil. If the spot still shows, remove the oil finish with pumice and water, dry thoroughly, and apply several more coats of varnish, following the steps under "Varnishing," Chapter X.

The varnish brush loses hairs.
New ox-hair brushes sometimes lose a few hairs the first or second time they are used. Before using, flick the hairs vigorously against a hard edge several times to remove any loose hairs. If the problem persists, the brush should be replaced.

REVERSE PAINTING ON GLASS (CHAPTER XI)

Etching does not cut through the gold leaf.
You have probably waited too long to do the etching. Gold leaf on glass can be etched as soon as it has dried and been burnished.

Etching is too light.
If the dark back-up paint has been applied but is not dry, an emergency measure that might be used is to remove the paint very carefully with turpentine. Since the gelatin size is water soluble, the turpentine should not affect the gold leaf unless it is rubbed too hard. This is recommended only if the etching is so unsatisfactory that the glass would not otherwise be used.

Finished tinsel painting has a spot that should be removed.
Mark the spot on the front of the glass with a piece of masking tape. Hold the glass to the light with the back toward you and scrape out the spot; repaint, if necessary.

Sandwich-edge Chippendale tray with Chinese motif. Black background; painted flowers and birds in border. Owned by Mrs. Nelson White. [Photo by Hubbard Phelps, Westerly, Rhode Island]

PART THREE

PATTERNS

Full-Size Patterns of
Early American Designs

AFTER STUDYING and developing some skill in the techniques of Early American decoration, the student will need patterns to work from if he is going to use his talents to produce copies of decorated antiques. The following collection includes some simple designs for the beginner and more complicated ones for the experienced decorator. Except for the mirror, each design was copied from an original or a copy of an original.

Originals are undoubtedly the best source of designs and some people who own them are very generous about lending them for the purpose of having the decoration recorded. Others prefer not to do this. Perhaps they feel that to have a number of copies in circulation would lessen the value of the article; but, actually, after an original has been copied and seen by many decorators, interest in the original increases and its value is amplified. Giving credit for ownership is sometimes difficult when copies have been copied a number of times, but it should be remembered that many of these decorated articles were produced in great quantity and therefore there are a number of duplicates still in existence.

Designs are frequently passed on to a succession of decorators, each of whom makes a change in the pattern. The latter copies, therefore, often have lost some of the character and detail of the originals. Working from black-and-white patterns is not ideal, but if the student has become familiar with the color mixtures, he should be able to produce fairly satisfactory copies.

The following explanations and references will help to keep the instructions simple and avoid repetition of the detailed directions already given.

The preparation and finishing of an article should be done according to the direc-

135]

FIGURE 24 *The proper brushes to use for the various strokes and techniques.*

tions found in Chapters VIII and X. Transferring a design to an article is explained in Chapter IX. The brushes used in each step are not mentioned, but as a general rule, square-tipped quills should be used for laying base coats, floating color, brush strokes, and dots. A long-pointed quill, or scroller, should be used for long, thin strokes; veins; stems; and large swirls. A short-pointed, red-sable watercolor brush can be

[*136*

used for curleycues, drips, tiny brush strokes, etc. A red-sable bright's brush is useful for blending two wet colors, foliage painting, and freehand bronzing. For flower painting, especially when using the wax medium, you will need a semifull-shaped, red-sable watercolor brush. Blending bronze powders in stenciling and freehand bronze can be done with short-pointed quills. (For additional information on the proper brushes to use in Early American decoration, see Figure 24.)

When orange-red is mentioned, you can use oil colors in English vermillion or cadmium red, light; japan colors, King Cole medium-orange or Signcraft red (in cans). Transparent yellow refers to either Indian yellow or yellow lake. When white is indicated, use striping white in japan—except for painting on glass, when oil colors are preferred. The country green, blue, and yellow in Plate 1 can be used as a median that can be designated as changing in hue or value. A size refers to any of those mentioned under "Picking the Proper Size" in Chapter V.

---

1. Painted base coat *Square-tipped quill, ¾ inch; Nos. 2, 3, 4, or 5, depending on the area to be covered.*

2. Country-tin strokes *Square-tipped quill, ¾ inch; Nos. 2, 3, or 4, depending on the size of the stroke.*

3. Drips, curleycues, and small scrolls *Scroller No. 1; and Finepoint, red-sable watercolor brush Nos. 1 or 2.*

4. Veins, long stems, and swirls *Scroller or long-pointed quill, Nos. 1 or 2.*

5. Stamens and fine crosshatching *Scroller No. 1.*

6. Large scrolls, sprays, etc. *Red-sable watercolor brush, semifull shape, Nos. 3, 4, or 5; or a square-tipped quill Nos. 2 or 3. Stems and fine lines Scroller or long-pointed quill, No. 1.*

7. Petal overlays *For Chippendale painting: red-sable watercolor brush, semifull shape, Nos. 4, 5, or 6; or square-tipped quill Nos. 2 or 3. For lace-edge painting: red-sable watercolor brush.*

8. Small flowers and dots *Square-tipped quill Nos. 2 or 3. For lace-edge painting: red-sable watercolor brush.*

9. Floating color on painted or stenciled base coat *Square-tipped quill, ¾ inch; Nos. 3, 4, or 5.*

10. Blending two wet colors *Square-tipped quill Nos. 3, 4, or 5; or red-sable bright's Nos. 7, 8, 9, or 10, depending on size of area being worked.*

11. Foliage *For initial strokes: square-tipped quill. For pulling down the stroke edge: red-sable bright's.*

PATTERN 1

Seamed coffin tray, 10½ by 15 inches (Figure 25)

1. Prepare the tray with a black background.

2. Trace the design and transfer to the tray. When the first half has been transferred, reverse the tracing and trace the other half.

3. Paint smooth orange-red base coats on the sixteen circles.

4. Mix chrome yellow medium, Prussian blue, raw umber, and a little white; and paint the groups of brush strokes. This color will be a bit lighter and more yellow than the country green.

5. When dry, paint the dark-red ovals over the circles with thin alizarin crimson and burnt umber.

6. Mix chrome yellow, medium, with a little raw umber and white, and paint thin overstrokes (indicated by broken lines) on the edges of the green strokes.

7. When dry, measure with a compass and white pencil the lengths of the strokes on the floor and flange of the tray. Paint the strokes freehand in the yellow mixture.

8. Paint in yellow: the fine crisscross lines in the centers of the groups of circles and the fine lines connecting the groups.

9. Paint the overstrokes (in broken lines) over the red ovals in semitransparent white.

10. Paint the red dots, stripe the tray on the edge in yellow, and finish the tray with handrubbing.

FIGURE 25 *Seamed coffin tray.* [*Photo by Charles Ferry*]

PATTERN I   *Tracing for seamed coffin tray (Figure 25).*

PATTERN 2

Bread tray with white band (Figure 26)

1. Prepare the tray with a black background.

2. Paint a white band around the edge (A), following the directions in Chapter IX.

3. When the band has been varnished and has dried, trace and transfer the design.

4. Paint one side of each leaf in orange-red (B).

5. Paint the other sides of the leaves with a mixture of Prussian blue, yellow ochre, and raw umber. Keep the mixture fairly thin so that the background will show through somewhat.

6. Paint the following in country yellow: the band on the floor (C), the ribbon-like brush strokes (D), the stripe on the inner side of the side bands, and the outside stripe around the tray.

7. Paint thin raw-umber strokes on the side of the ribbon strokes. With black enamel or seal, paint the veins on the leaves, the curleycues, the wavy line on the center band, and the large dot and brush strokes between the two large leaves.

8. Finish with handrubbing.

FIGURE 26 *Portion of bread tray, showing design.* [*Photo by Charles Ferry*]

PATTERN 2   *Tracing for bread tray (Figure 26).*

Pattern 3

Large box

I have had this pattern for a number of years, but I am uncertain as to exactly what sort of box it was found on. It is adaptable to several types of articles and is unusual because it includes a purple shade not often found in country painting.

1. Prepare the article with a black or asphaltum background.

2. Trace the design and transfer it to the article.

3. Paint all the solid-black areas in country green with a tiny bit of white added. On D paint a spot of white where indicated by the dotted circle, and blend the edges. (See "Blending Two Wet Colors" in Chapter II.)

4. The fruit marked A and B are painted alike, but they must be painted one at a time and blended while wet so that there is no line between the two colors. A sections are a mixture of orange-red and a little burnt umber. B sections are country yellow.

5. The grapes (C-1 and C-2) are a medium gray-purple (Prussian blue, alizarin crimson, white, and raw umber). Paint the plum (C-3) in the same color and add a spot of white within the dotted oval. Blend into the purple.

6. Paint all remaining unlettered strokes, grapes, and stems in country yellow.

7. Paint yellow strokes on the five individual grapes (C-1) and on the edges of the leaves within the white outlines. Paint one yellow stroke on the middle of the three large leaves.

8. On the large area representing a bunch of grapes (C-2), paint the strokes with a solid outline in thin alizarin crimson, and those with a broken outline in thin white. The dots are yellow.

9. Paint thin black veins in the leaves and strokes where indicated, and a black line on the yellow center veins.

10. Finish with handrubbing.

Pattern 3   *Tracing of country painting for large box.*

PATTERN 4

Tin trunk, No. 1

1. Prepare the trunk with a black background.
2. Trace the design and transfer to the front panel.
3. Paint all sections marked A with a mixture of orange-red and a little burnt umber. When painting the buds, cover a complete oval, disregarding the green strokes which are painted over the red when it is dry.
4. Paint all solid-black areas in country green.
5. Paint remaining strokes in country yellow with a little less umber.
6. When these layers are dry, paint thin white overstrokes on the flowers and buds where indicated.
7. Paint a yellow brush stroke on the edge of each of the large green brush strokes and the veins in the leaves.
8. Paint yellow brush strokes on the top and ends of the trunk (see Pattern 5b), stripe in yellow, and finish with handrubbing or semigloss varnish.

*Papier-mâché Gothic tray with gold-leaf scrolls
and painted flowers. Owned by Rose Nichols.*
[*From* The Ornamented Tray]

PATTERN 4 *Tracing of design for tin trunk No. 1.*

PATTERNS 5a AND 5b

Tin trunk, No. 2 (Figure 27)

1. Prepare the trunk with an asphaltum background.

2. Paint a white band at A (Pattern 5a), according to directions given in Chapter IX. Paint an orange-red band at B.

3. Trace the design, and transfer it to the front panel which has been varnished and dried.

4. Paint all orange-red units (C).

5. Paint all solid-black areas in country green (with a bluish tone). The strokes on the white band can be painted with a little thinner mixture.

6. In country yellow, paint the birds and the remaining strokes that have a solid outline.

7. When dry, paint overstrokes of thin alizarin crimson and burnt umber on units C that are painted on the asphaltum ground (solid outlines). Paint thin white strokes (broken outlines) when the red is dry.

8. Paint thin white strokes on the leaves within the white outlines and also on the background within the broken outlines.

FIGURE 27 *Design (asphaltum background) for tin trunk No. 2. [Photo by Fred Kent]*

PATTERN 5a   *Tracing of design for tin trunk No. 2 (Figure 27).*

PATTERN 5b *Stroke designs for tin trunk No. 2 (Figure 27).*

9. Paint a stroke of bright yellow along the edges of the birds' breasts and blend toward the center with clear varnish.

10. Paint the following in black: the wavy line and the stripe on the red band; strokes; eyes of birds; circles of small dots on red circles; and larger dots at the base. Stems are white.

11. In the band design, paint in black: a narrow stroke on the upper edge of each green stroke (D); strokes, lines, and dots on the red flowers; stems; and fine cross-lines.

12. Paint in yellow: the strokes above the white band, the two stripes under these, and the stripes boxing in the design below the white band.

13. Paint strokes on top and ends (Pattern 5b) in country yellow. Box in the ends (A) with striping. The pattern for the top (B) includes the stroke and border designs that go around the handle. Strokes C represent the pattern for the top border.

14. Stripe and finish with handrubbing or semigloss varnish.

PATTERN 6

Oval tea caddy (Figure 28)

1. Prepare the tea caddy with a black background.

2. Trace the design and transfer to the caddy (the wreath on top and the garland around the sides).

3. Paint soft-coral base coats (white, orange-red, yellow ochre, and burnt umber) on the two large flowers. Cover the entire flower, including the brush strokes at the bottom and the outlined oval at the top.

4. Add a bit of white and raw umber to country green and paint the solid-black strokes.

5. Paint the small flowers (A) in orange-red; and the others (B) in white, with a little raw umber.

6. Paint all remaining strokes in pale yellow (white, chrome yellow medium, and burnt umber).

7. Paint the ribbon in country blue, and when dry, add white overstrokes where indicated.

8. Paint the heavily outlined ovals on the flowers in transparent alizarin crimson and burnt umber, and let dry; then thin the base coat color and use it to paint small strokes around the top edge.

9. When dry, paint semitransparent overstrokes (C and D) which were outlined in Step 8. To assure the proper position, the broken line shows the outline of the flower.

10. The wreath of strokes for the top of the caddy is orange-red (solid black) and white (outlined).

11. Add white stripes above and below the garland decoration, and finish with handrubbing.

FIGURE 28 *Design for oval tea caddy.* [*Photo by Fred Kent*]

PATTERN 6   Tracing of design for oval tea caddy (Figure 28).

PATTERN 7

Stenciled box (Figure 29)

1. Prepare the box with an asphaltum background. Keep it thin enough to look coppery.

2. Trace the stencil on architects' linen. Cut the top stencil completely; or cut only two sides and move the stencil around the box to complete the other two sides.

3. Varnish the box, and when tacky, apply the stencils, using rich-gold bronze powder. All the designs, except the two large flowers, are done in solid gold. Shade these slightly to give the effect of a faint shadow just inside the lower edge.

4. Stripe with country yellow and finish with handrubbing or semigloss varnish

FIGURE 29   *Stenciled box, courtesy of Miss Frances Jette, Montpelier, Vermont; Chippendale tray owned by author; bellows, courtesy* *of Mrs. Robert Bliss, Montpelier, Vermont.* [*Photo by Fred Kent*]

PATTERN 7 *Stencils for metal box shown in lower left-hand corner of Figure 29.*

PATTERNS 8a AND 8b

Pictorial handhold tray, 12 by 15 inches (Figure 30)

1. Trace the stencils on Pattern 8a on architects' linen, leaving at least an inch around each unit. Cut the stencils.

2. Prepare the tray with a black background.

3. Stripe the tray after drawing guidelines with a compass and white pencil. The fine inside stripe on the floor encloses an area approximately 7 by 10½ inches. About ⅛ inch nearer the turn of the tray is a wider (3/16 inch) stripe and then another fine stripe. These are done in deep-gold powder. The fine stripe just inside the edge of the flange is yellow.

4. When dry, varnish the tray; then, when tacky, apply the stencil units—all in solid-silver powder—in this order: girl, bird, dog, flower.

5. Stencil in deep gold: the fence (blending the powder off behind the bird and the girl), the tree trunk (leaving a shadow on one side), and the overlapping leaf units.

6. With a brush or velvet, rub some deep-gold powder under the bird and the dog, and around the girl's feet, to represent the ground.

7. Wash off the loose powder and varnish the tray.

8. When dry, apply the washes of transparent color. The girl's dress, the spots on her cheeks, the flowers on her hat, and the bird's tail are alizarin crimson. The

FIGURE 30 *Pictorial tray with handholes.*
[*Photo by Fred Kent*]

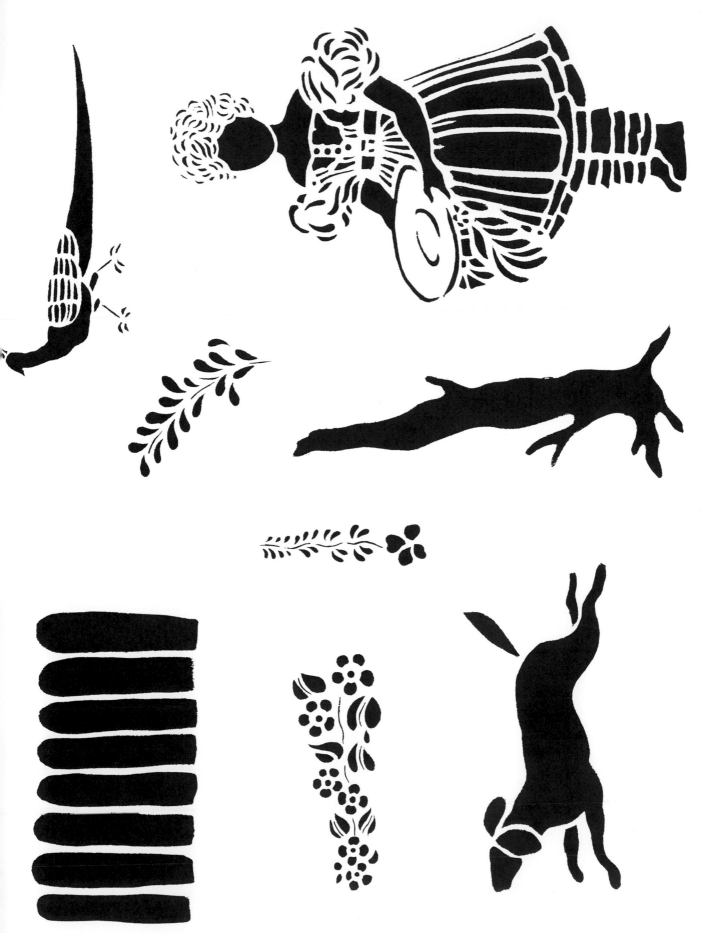

PATTERN 8a   *Stencil units for pictorial tray (Figure 30).*

PATTERN 8b   *Border design for pictorial tray (Figure 30).*

bird's head and breast are green (Prussian blue and transparent yellow) blended down to raw umber under the wing. The leaves on the hat held by the girl are green. Float a wash of thin burnt umber over the entire dog; while this is still wet, paint a spot of alizarin crimson and burnt umber on his back, and blend the edges. Paint the same color on his ears. The flower units are thin alizarin crimson at the tops, blended to nothing toward the bottom. Paint the girl's features in black.

9. Paint the foliage with a side-loaded brush, as shown in Figure 12. The foliage above the fence is a country green; that below and to the right of the fence is a more yellow green; and a mixture of burnt sienna and yellow ochre is used in the lower left corner and middle.

10. Trace the border design (8b), and transfer it to the flange. The half shown in the tracing can be moved around to complete the opposite side.

11. Paint the leaves in country green; when dry, paint the curleycues and stems in the same color.

12. When the green is dry, paint the center veins in chrome yellow, medium; and the side veins with a mixture of rich-gold powder and varnish.

13. Clean the tray and finish with handrubbing.

PATTERNS 9a, 9b, AND 9c

Handhole tray with boat scene, 20½ by 28 inches (Figure 31)

1. Prepare the tray with a black background.

2. Draw guidelines for the stripes (Pattern 9a) and paint them in yellow enamel. The inside stripe is about ⅞ inch from the turn of the tray. The other three are on the flange—one at the base; and the other two ½ inch and ¼ inch, respectively, from the edge. When the enamel is tacky, rub on pale-gold bronze powder.

3. When dry, wash off excess powder, dust the flange with talcum powder, and transfer the border design (Patterns 9a and 9b) to the tray.

4. Paint the two roses and large leaves in black enamel or seal; and when tacky, apply XX gold leaf as directed in Chapter V.

5. Brush off the loose gold leaf, and paint the remainder of the design in red or yellow enamel. If the enamel dries too fast, add a little varnish or gold size. When tacky, apply gold leaf.

6. Brush off the loose gold, and etch the roses and leaves as indicated.

7. Trace the stencils (Pattern 9b) on architects' linen and cut the solid-black portions. The ship stencil is a silhouette, so after cutting the black areas (ignore the broken lines as they are painted in afterward), cut out the ship on the black outline.

FIGURE 31 *Boat-scene tray with handholes.*
[*Photo by Charles Ferry*]

PATTERN 9a *Border design (partial) for large tray with boat scene (Figure 31).*

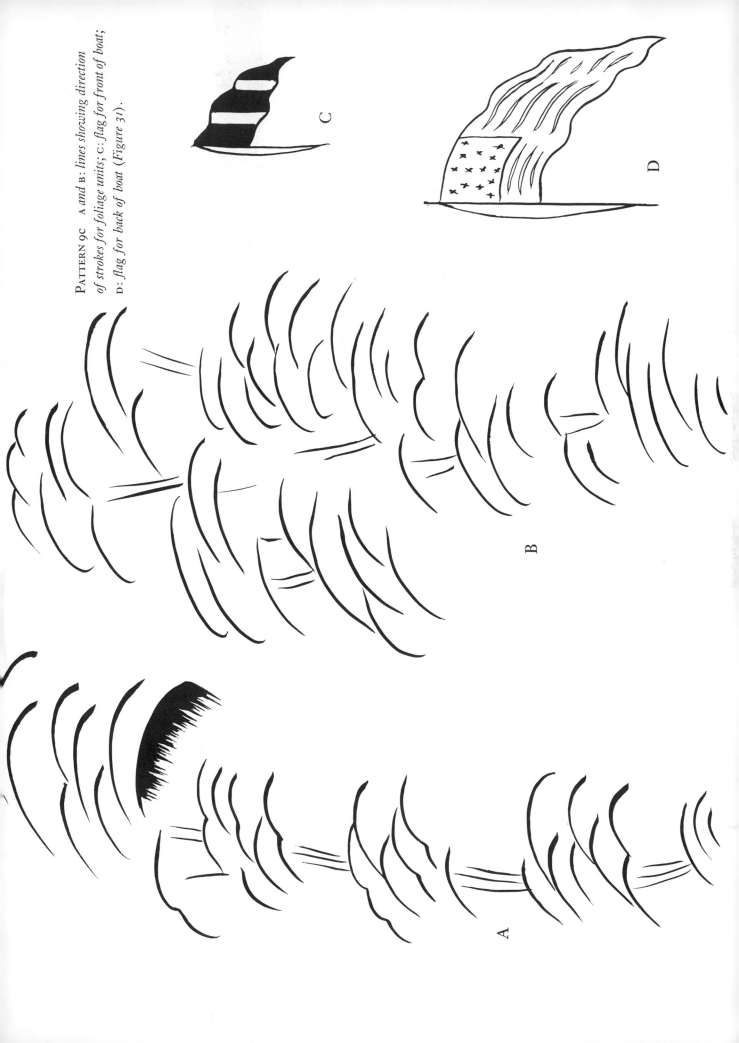

PATTERN 9C   A and B: *lines showing direction of strokes for foliage units*; C: *flag for front of boat*; D: *flag for back of boat (Figure 31)*.

Bread tray with gold-leaf decoration. [Courtesy of the Cooper Union Museum, New York, New York]

8. When the gold-leaf units are dry, varnish the entire tray; when tacky, apply the stencils in silver powder. In case your tray is not the same size as the one illustrated, before varnishing, block out with chalk a rectangle about 17½ by 11 inches. The ship is placed so that the upper left corner of the stencil is about 2 inches from the left side of the rectangle and 6 inches from the top.

9. Stencil the boat and sky solidly in silver powder, blending off rather abruptly at the top edge of the sky. Lay a straight edge of linen on the horizon line to the right of the boat so that the sky area ends sharply. Stencil the water less solidly in silver, and blend off gradually at the bottom and sides.

10. Six flower stencils appear in a sort of semicircle around the bottom of the water. (See stencil for these flowers in Pattern 9b.) Located about 1½ to 2 inches apart, they are stenciled heavily in the middle, but fade off so that their edges are not visible. Three or four other flower stencils appear more faintly below these.

11. Cut a straight edge and curve (which follows the corner turn of the tray) on linen, and lay it just beyond the inside stripe. Stencil the edge in silver, blending out toward the turn, and move the linen around the tray to make a continuous edge.

12. When dry, wash the stencil and varnish the tray.

13. When the varnish is dry, trace the two flags (Pattern 9c) and transfer them to the tray in the proper positions. (See Figure 31.) Paint the one on the left (C) with alternating stripes of black, and alizarin crimson with burnt umber. On the other flag (D), the field is alizarin crimson and burnt umber, and the rest is Prussian blue and raw umber. When these are dry, paint the stars in country yellow and the stripes in white with raw umber. A stroke of thin raw umber where the outline dips will give an impression of folds.

14. Paint the clouds and puffs of smoke with black seal thinned with varnish. Add the black lines (D) and the white lines (E), which are indicated in Pattern 9b by the broken lines.

15. Float a thin Prussian blue wash on the water, adding a bit of transparent yellow nearer the boat to give the water a greenish hue. Paint a few white brush strokes at the water line to resemble whitecaps. The flowers are thin alizarin crimson at the top blended down to nothing.

16. Trace the guidelines for the foliage (Pattern 9c) and transfer to the tray with A to the left and B to the right. Trace some of the strokes along the bottom, filling in among the flowers and completing the rectangle. Paint the foliage, following the directions in Chapter III.

17. Finish the tray with handrubbing.

PATTERNS 10a AND 10b

Tray with fruit-and-flower basket, 17 by 22 inches (Figure 32)

This tray had no visible border design, but one could very easily be added by means of simple striping or a repeat stencil.

1. Prepare the tray with a black background, and stripe.

2. Trace the stencils (Pattern 10a) on architects' linen, leaving at least an inch around each unit. Cut the stencils.

3. Varnish the tray, and when tacky, apply the stencils. The stenciled design occupies an oval space about 7 by 9 inches. Place the basket in the center about 2 inches from the bottom and stencil in silver. Stencil the grapes in rich gold, blending off at the edges. All other units are stenciled in silver with shading where indicated.

4. With a stump, put in the silver highlights under the basket; then rub in a deep-gold oval with velvet or a brush, blending off at the edges.

5. When dry, wash off the excess powder and varnish the tray.

6. When the varnish is thoroughly dry, apply the color washes: Basket—very thin alizarin crimson. Grapes—thin alizarin crimson over entire bunch, then a deeper shade with a bit of Prussian blue added on the edges. Pineapple and small flowers—

FIGURE 32 *Though this has no border design, one could easily be added.* [*Photo by Fred Kent*]

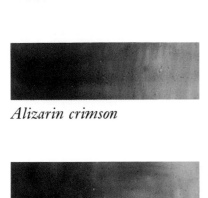

Alizarin crimson

Indian yellow
Raw umber

Alizarin crimson
Burnt umber

Indian yellow
Burnt umber

Alizarin crimson
Indian yellow

Prussian blue

Alizarin crimson
Prussian blue

Prussian blue
Raw umber

Indian yellow or
Yellow lake

Prussian blue
Indian yellow

Indian yellow
Alizarin crimson

Prussian blue
Alizarin crimson

Indian yellow
Prussian blue

PLATE 9 Colors and mixtures used in Chippendale painting. Transparent and semitransparent, they are shaded from deep (less varnish used) to pale (more varnish used). When mixing the above, start with the first color indicated and add a small amount of the second color.

PLATE 10 Step-by-step paintings of Chippendale-type flowers: (A) blue daisy; (B) blue pods; (C) small red flower; (D) white daisy; (E) passion flower; (F) morning glory; and (G) fuchsia.

PATTERN 10a   *Stencil units for tray with fruit-and-flower basket (Figure 32).*

P ATTERN 10b   *Tracings of strokes surrounding fruit-and-flower basket (Figure 32).*

thin green (Prussian blue and transparent yellow). Large flowers—deep Prussian blue on top petals blended to nothing in the centers.

7. When the color has dried, trace the painted border design (Pattern 10b). This has been drawn in two sections. First trace the curve from A (solid outline) to broken line B. Next trace from broken line A to B (solid outline), fitting the two As and Bs together. Transfer the tracing to the tray and paint the large strokes in country green.

8. The solid-black strokes, stems, swirls, and fine lines are country yellow.

9. Finish the tray with handrubbing.

PATTERNS 11a AND 11C

Small Boston rocker (Figure 33)

1. Prepare the rocker with a black or rosewood-grained background (see Chapter VIII).

2. Cut a piece of architects' linen the shape of the chair back and lay it over the top stencil (Pattern 11a), centering the unit. Trace the design and then lay the linen over the lower stencils, matching the As and Bs on the right and left. Trace the two stencils C and D for the leaf veins on separate pieces of linen and cut all the stencils.

3. Varnish the chair back and when tacky, apply the stencil, using rich-gold powder with a little deep gold in the centers of the rose cups. Blend the lower petals at the edges to give form to the flower. Stencil the leaves heavily on the edges and tips, and blend off toward the centers. Stencil vein C on all curved leaves (it will have to be reversed for some leaves) and vein D on the large middle leaf.

4. Stencil the roll (the front edge of the seat) with one of the designs in Pattern 11c.

5. Stripe the back with one wide ($\frac{3}{16}$ inch) and one fine stripe in deep gold. Stripe the rest of the chair in country yellow, as suggested in Pattern 12c.

6. When dry, finish with semigloss varnish.

FIGURE 33 *Designs for top slats of small* (BELOW) *and large* (ABOVE) *Boston rockers.* [*Photo by Charles Ferry*]

PATTERN 11a *Stencils for top slat of small Boston rocker (Figure 33).*

PATTERN 11b

Large Boston rocker (Figure 33)

1. Prepare the rocker with a black or rosewood background.

2. Trace the five stencil units on architects' linen, leaving an ample margin around each, and cut them.

3. Varnish the chair back, and when tacky, use rich-gold powder to stencil the eagle solidly, except for the body which can be shaded off at the edges to give it form. Lay the leaf unit to the left of the eagle and stencil, blending leaf A where it goes behind the wing tip. The leaves are rich gold and the berries are silver.

4. Clean the leaf stencil, reverse it, and lay it to the right of the eagle. Stencil all but berries B, which can then be moved nearer the flag to position C and stenciled. Stencil stars D on the shield, stars E on the flag, and branches F beneath the eagle's claws.

5. Apply one of the roll stencils (Pattern 11c) and stripe.

6. When the stenciling and striping is dry, varnish and allow to dry. Float a wash of thin green (Prussian blue and transparent yellow) on the leaves, and when dry, add a stroke of burnt umber. Paint thin burnt umber just under each row of feathers and around the outer edge of the bird's body.

7. Finish with semigloss varnish.

PATTERN 11c *Stencils for rolls of Boston rockers.*

Reproductions of trays with painting and free-hand bronzing on gold-leaf bands.

Gallery tray with portrait medallion. [*Courtesy of the* Cooper Union Museum, New York, New York]

PATTERN 11b   *Stencils for top slat of large Boston rocker (Figure 33).*

PATTERNS 12a, 12b, AND 12c

Fiddleback chair (Figures 34 and 35)

This is an especially handsome fiddleback chair with unusual legs—ordinarily they are of the Hitchcock type. There is no striping except on the top slat.

1. Prepare the chair with a rosewood-grained background.

2. Trace on linen and cut the 24 stencil units (Patterns 12a and 12b), leaving ample margins around the units.

3. Varnish the top slat, and when tacky, apply the stencils in the following order:

A—Rich gold, solidly on the stem, the two side strokes; and on the other three shapes, blending toward the center.

B—Rich gold, blending off under the overlapping units.

C—Rich gold, blending off under the overlapping units.

D—Rich gold.

R—Deep gold above and below the center unit.

H—Deep gold, with rich-gold veins shaded as indicated. This leaf should be cut like the one in Figure 9.

FIGURE 34 *Fiddleback chair, courtesy of Mrs. W. K. Howe, North Andover, Massachusetts.*

PATTERN 12a   *Stencil units (partial) for fiddleback chair*
(Figures 34 and 35).

O

P

Q

R

S

W

T

V

U

X

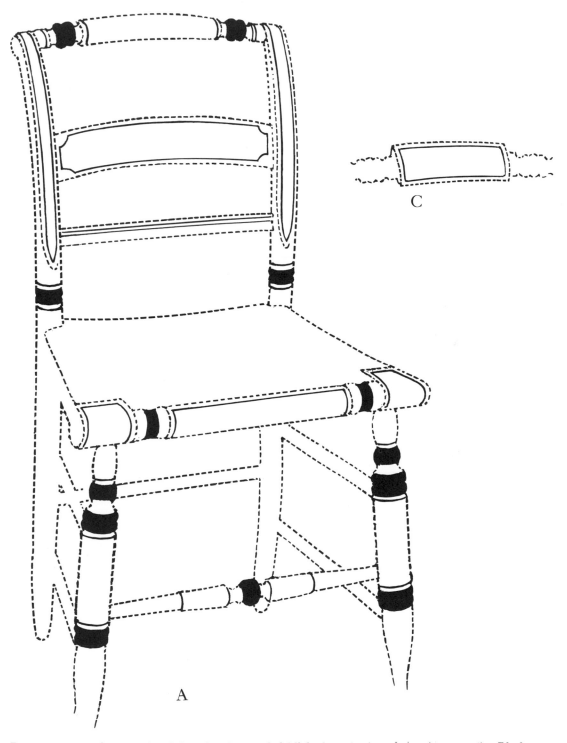

C

A

PATTERN 12c *Suggested striping for decorated fiddleback and other chairs (page 178). Black bands are gold; solid lines are country yellow. Shown are (A) bolster-back Hitchcock; (B) Boston rocker; and (C) pillow-back for Hitchcock.*

PATTERN 12b *Remaining stencil units for fiddleback chair (Figures 34 and 35).*

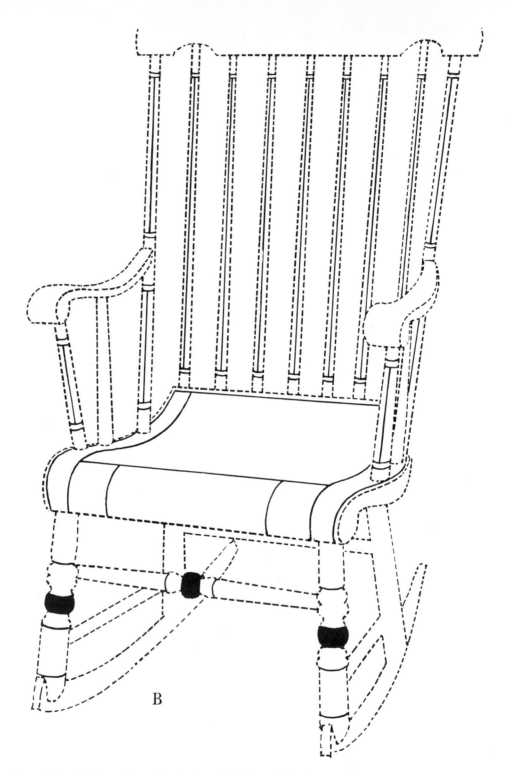

B

E and F—Rich gold to the left and right of the leaves.
I and J—Rich gold at the right and left ends of the slat. Fill in with separate grapes.
L—Leaves and seeds in rich gold, and the strawberry in deep gold.
G, K, M, and N—Rich gold where shown.

4. Varnish the center slat and when tacky, apply the stencils in the following order:

O and Q—Deep gold at bottom and top of slat.

U—Rich gold first; then smudge deep gold in the openings and below the basket.

S—Rich gold to the left of the basket handle. Stencil from the edge at three equidistant places on the circle and blend off toward the center. With a stump or bob, make three strokes from the center out. Repeat the procedure above and to the left.

V—Rich gold, with deep gold added to places where highlight blends into shadow.

T, X, and N—Rich gold, placed and shaded as indicated.

K and L—Stencil as on the top slat where indicated. For the leaf, use the tip of H.

5. The stripe can be stenciled or painted. If stenciled, cut the proper curves on linen and stencil in deep gold. If painted, wash the slats and varnish. Let dry thoroughly; then dust the area lightly with talcum powder, and with a wide quill striper or a sword striper paint the stripe in yellow enamel thinned with a little varnish. When tacky, rub on deep-gold powder.

6. Varnish the stiles and roll; when tacky, apply stencils P and W in rich gold. The white lines on P can be painted in black when the stencil is dry.

7. Clean, and finish with semigloss varnish.

FIGURE 35 *Detail of top and back slats of fiddleback chair shown in Figure 34. [Photo by Fred Kent]*

179]

PATTERNS 13a, 13b, 13c, AND 13d

Large tray, 20 by 28 inches (Figure 36)

1. Prepare the tray with a red background. Lowe Brothers' Plax in Oriental red (velvet finish) was used on the tray shown in Figure 36.

2. Draw guidelines and stripe the tray. Use rich-gold powder on enamel paint. The center stripes form a rectangle 7 by 15 inches.

3. On architects' linen trace the 14 stencil units on Patterns 13a, 13b, and 13c that are solid black, and cut.

4. Cut a piece of tracing paper about 7 by 16 inches, lay it over A (Pattern 13a) and trace the solid outlines. From Pattern 13d, fit D to the left and C to the right of A, and trace. Transfer this design to the two ends of the tray, including the flange.

5. Cut a piece of tracing paper 7 by 22 inches, and lay the right end over B (Pattern 13d). Trace the outlines, then lay the tracing over F (Pattern 13b), fitting the grapes together. Now trace this outline and lay the left end over E (Pattern 13d), fitting the solid to the broken outlines. Trace these outlines and transfer the entire tracing to the long sides of the tray.

6. All these designs must now be painted with black seal. The black base coats must be very smooth to receive the bronze powder, so they must be painted rather quickly. Start with one of the smaller end designs. Use a No. 5 square-tipped quill, load the brush well, and dress it in the center of the design rather than on the palette. This will cover a fair amount of the center section. Work out to the edges in all directions to keep any of the edges from setting up. If you have trouble covering such a large area without getting ridges, try using some black enamel with slow gold size or Walter Wright's mixture, substituting black for yellow enamel (see Chapter V, "Picking the Proper Size").

7. Except for the stump work, all the stenciling and freehand bronzing is done in rich-gold powder. Apply stencils 9, 12, and 13 (Pattern 13a) where indicated by the broken lines. Use one of the curves in stencil 9 to outline the pear. Shade the fruit to give it form. Rub bronze powder on the edges of the leaves and blend off toward the center. Stencil veins 5 and 6 (Pattern 13b) and add stump work in silver between the outer veins. Stencil the small leaves as shown. Apply stencil 1 (Pattern 13a) to flower D (Pattern 13d) and shade from the tips of the petals to the base.

8. Paint one of the side designs on the tray in black. This is larger than the end design, and if covering the whole area in one step presents a problem, there are opportunities here to end some sections along the broken lines where the edge of a stencil will fall. Avoid ridges along the edges.

9. When the size has reached the proper tack, apply stencil 10 (Pattern 13c) in its proper place. Make two highlights on the main part, and stencil the crescent section from the top, blending off toward the point. Next stencil all the grapes that show completely. These are all the large-size ones (3z in Pattern 13a) which are

[*180*

PLATE 11   Step-by-step paintings of three types of Chippendale roses.

PLATE 12   Typical lace-edge flowers, leaf, and border designs.

9

13

12

A

PATTERN 13a Stencil units 1–3 and tracing of end design for large tray with freehand-bronze design (Figure 36).

PATTERN 13b *Stencil units 4–6 and partial tracing of side design in Figure 36.*

PATTERN 13C *Stencil units 7–14 for Figure 36.*

FIGURE 36 *Handhole tray with freehand bronze and stenciled design. [Photo by Charles Ferry]*

indicated by broken lines on Patterns 13b and 13d). Stencil these with a highlight just under the top edge and a reflected light along the bottom edge. Stencil stems 14 (Pattern 13d) and fill in with the other grapes (3x and 3y on Patterns 13b and 13d).

10. Next stencil 7 and 11 (Pattern 13c). Blend off the melon behind the grapes and cut a small outside curve to produce the hard edge in 11. Stencil dots (8) along the ridges of the melon to give it texture. Rub powder on the bird's head and tail, and stencil the tips of the wings (stencil 2, Pattern 13a). Lay stencil 4 (Pattern 13b) on E (Pattern 13d) and blend powder from the tips of the petals to the base. Paint the curleycues and the bird's eye in black.

11. Finish with handrubbing.

PATTERN 13d *Tracings for completing end and side designs of Figure 36.*

PATTERN 14

Theorem (fruit painting on velvet) [*Figure 37*]

1. Prepare the velvet as described in Chapter III.
2. Cut three pieces of architects' linen the size of the velvet, and trace on piece 1 all the solid-black areas, on piece 2 all the outlined areas, and on piece 3 all the shaded areas.
3. Cut the three stencils.
4. Tape the first piece of linen in place and stencil the leaves in green (Prussian blue and transparent yellow), adding burnt sienna on some of the tips and edges. Stencil the pear, leaving the outlined spot in the tracing untouched to effect a highlight. On the right side, use a bluish green that turns to yellow-green before reaching the highlight. On the left side, stencil in burnt umber and alizarin crimson, blending off toward the center. Stencil the raspberries with alizarin crimson, applying it heavily on the right sides and bottoms.
5. Remove stencil 1 and tape stencil 2 in place, adjusting the register. The pear is burnt umber on the right side, with yellow near the center; the left side is alizarin crimson, with just a bit of burnt umber. Stencil the leaves as you did the first ones (Step 4), with variations in shade and value.
6. Remove stencil 2 and tape on stencil 3. The branches are burnt umber, heavier on the underside. The rest is green.
7. The rest of the design is executed with a pointed brush moistened in turpentine. The stems and veins are raw umber. The lines on the raspberries are dark alizarin crimson.

FIGURE 37 *Fruit painting on velvet (theorem).* [*Photo by Fred Kent*]

[*186*

PATTERN 14 *Stencil separations and tracing for fruit theorem (Figure 37).*

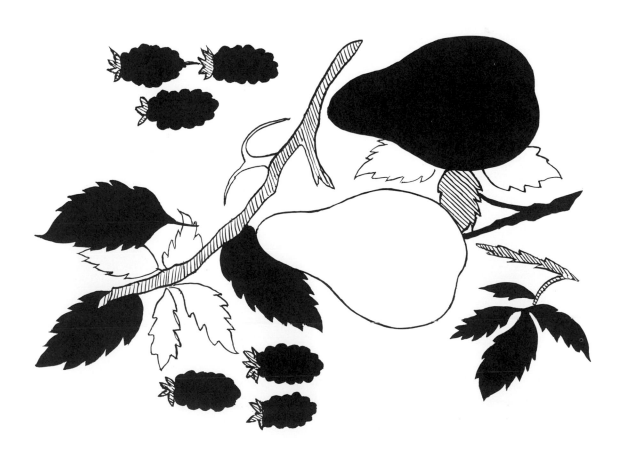

PATTERNS 15a AND 15b

Theorem (flower painting on velvet) [Figure 38]

1. Prepare the velvet as described in Chapter III.
2. Cut four pieces of architects' linen the size of the velvet. Lay one over the

FIGURE 38 *Flower painting on velvet (theorem). Courtesy of Mrs. Ralph Holmes, Plaistow, New Hampshire.*

PATTERN 15a   *Stencil separations for flower theorem (Figure 38).*

189]

PATTERN 15b *Tracing of design for flower theorem (Figure 38).*

separations tracing (Pattern 15a) and trace all the solid-black sections. Remove this piece of linen; then trace the other three sections—outlined, shaded, and crisscross—on the other three linen pieces, using one piece of linen for each section.

3. Cut the four stencils. The two areas in the morning glories marked X are not stencils, but are part of the velvet background.

4. The colors used for the various flowers and leaves are listed below. The values, or depths, of color can be determined by studying the photograph of the finished velvet. Although purists do not use white for work on velvet, Mrs. Holmes, the painter of Figure 38, did add a little white to the pale colors in order to achieve more of a three-dimensional effect on the toned velvet. If you are working with a limited palette, it would be wise to experiment with different mixtures on a practice piece of velvet.

Fuchsias—Alizarin crimson, from pale to deep tones. Overstrokes are the same.

Morning glories—Thalo blue with a little titanium white. Add some alizarin crimson at areas marked A on the tracing (Pattern 15b). Cut a curve on linen, and stencil at B in green (Prussian blue and transparent yellow), changing quickly to yellow for the rest of the opening. The small stroke is outlined in raw umber. The funnel is very pale green-blue, with burnt-umber shadows.

Lilies—Venetian red with a little white in very delicate shades. Overstrokes are Venetian red and alizarin crimson; the stamens are raw umber.

Campanulas—Very pale green, with light applications of burnt umber on either side of the funnel. Under the outer petals at C, a deep-purple shade similar to A quickly blends to nothing toward the outer edge. The tiny stamen is alizarin crimson.

Pansy—Petals F are deep alizarin crimson at the center, blending to pale purple at the top. In order to get a rich-purple tone you may have to use a tube color such as cobalt violet. The other three petals are alizarin crimson on the edges with very faint purple; and toward the center, a little yellow. Use alizarin crimson for overstrokes.

Leaves—Green, shading from yellow-greens to blue-greens, obtained by mixing various proportions of Prussian blue with transparent yellow. Use veridian for brighter greens. Leaves D are yellowish toward the center. Use an edge of linen to get the sharp separations from one value to another. On leaves E, burnt umber has been worked in where the letter appears on the tracing. Leaf F is yellow on the tip.

Fine lines—Veins, stems, and curleycues are raw umber, with a bit of Prussian blue. The fine, light lines on the flowers are done in umber with a bit of the native color added; the only exceptions are the lines in the morning glories that are on the velvet background and that follow the curve of the petals—these are done in alizarin crimson.

PATTERNS 16a, 16b, 16c, 16d, 16e, AND 16f

Wall stencil (Figure 39)

These stencils were found on the walls of an old inn in western New York State by Mrs. William Schwab of Gainesville, New York. The frieze stencil A (Pattern 16a); vertical borders B, C, and D (Patterns 16b and 16c); and the eagle stencil (Patterns 16d and 16e) decorated the walls of the ballroom in a panel design. In another room, the frieze border H (Pattern 16f) was used with two eagles, as well as with border D, on which the three birds were perched at intervals. The stencils are rather crude, but they are simple to work with and quite effective.

1. Prepare the walls, trace and cut the stencils, and apply them in the desired combinations, following the directions given in Chapter III. Outlined areas of different colors must be cut separately and applied over the first stencil.

2. The colors used for these stencils are red (orange-red with a little white and burnt sienna); green (chrome yellow, medium; Prussian blue; and a little of the red mixture); blue (white, Prussian blue, and a little raw umber); and black.

FIGURE 39   *Stencils on the walls of an old inn in western New York State. Photographed by Mrs. William Schwab, Gainesville, New York.*

PATTERN 16a   *Tracing of frieze border shown in wall stencil with single eagle (Figure 39).*

PATTERN 16b *Tracing of units in vertical borders of single-eagle wall stencil (Figure 39).*

PATTERN 16C   *Tracings of units for center designs in wall stencils (Figure 39).*

PATTERN 16d   *Tracing of left side of eagle (Figure 39).*

PATTERN 16e   *Tracing of right side of eagle (Figure 39).*

3. In frieze border A (Pattern 16a), the colors are green (1) and black (2) with dots. In vertical border B (Pattern 16b), the colors are green (1) and black (2). Border C (Pattern 16b) is all green. In Border D (Pattern 16c), the leaves are green and the flowers red. Bird E is green; bird F is blue, with a red wing and headpiece; and bird G is red, with a black wing and headpiece. Eyes can be painted in with black. In border H (Pattern 16f), the crescents are green, the upper flowers (1) are red and the alternate ones (2) green. The eagle (Patterns 16d and 16e) is green, but it was difficult to determine the color of the overlay stencil (lettering, and the strokes on body and wings). Though it seemed to be white, it showed up on the light wall; so enough umber could be added to provide a contrast.

PATTERN 16f *Tracing of frieze border shown in wall stencil with two eagles and birds (Figure 39).*

PATTERN 17

Metal box with gold-leaf and freehand-bronze decoration (Figure 40)

1. Prepare the box with a black background.
2. Trace the design and transfer it to the box.
3. Paint all leaves A with black enamel or seal (be sure to dust talcum powder on the area), and when tacky, apply XX gold leaf, as described in Chapter V.
4. Brush off the loose gold, and etch where indicated.
5. Mix a grayed blue-green and paint leaves B and C, using enough varnish to produce a smooth base coat which will become tacky. When the paint has reached the proper tack, rub bronze powder on the edges and blend off toward the center. On leaves B use Butler's silver or aluminum powder toned down with a small amount of gold bronze powder. On leaves C apply deep-gold powder in the same way.
6. In yellow size, paint all the small black strokes and the stems; when tacky, rub on the bronze powder used on leaves B.
7. Paint the stripes in yellow size, and when tacky, rub on deep-gold powder. Your box may not be the same proportions as the one shown here, but enclose the

FIGURE 40 *Metal box with gold-leaf and freehand-bronze decoration. Courtesy of Mrs. H. A. Prym, Thompson, Connecticut.*

PATTERN 17 *Tracing of design for metal box (Figure 40).*

cover design with one fine and one wide stripe, and the border design with two wide stripes.

8. Wash off the excess powder and varnish the box.

9. If the flowers have disappeared after the varnish has dried, retrace them; then paint them in white, with a touch of raw umber.

10. When the flowers are dry, apply the color washes. On flowers D the color on the edges where the letter appears is deep Prussian blue, blended off toward the center. On flowers E the blue wash is continued around the flower, leaving only the center clear. Flowers F are treated like D with a lighter alizarin crimson and burnt-umber wash. On flowers G the crimson wash around the edges of the flowers is much lighter so that the whole flower is visible.

11. When all the floated color is dry, varnish the box and dry for at least a week.

12. Dust a thin layer of talcum powder over the flowers, paint the round centers in enamel or seal, and when tacky, apply gold leaf. Brush off the loose gold.

13. Outline the gold centers in black; then add black dots to the flowers on the cover and black ovals on the border flowers. Paint all the fine black lines on the flowers, and the veins on the green leaves. Paint burnt-umber strokes on the gold-leaf leaves where indicated by the shaded strokes on sample leaves.

14. When thoroughly dry, finish with handrubbing or semigloss varnish.

PATTERN 18

Turtleback bellows, design No. 1 (Figure 41)

I have included two designs for bellows because they provide a good opportunity to work in both gold leaf and freehand bronze. The designs are also adaptable to other articles.

FIGURE 41 *Turtleback bellows with gold-leaf and freehand-bronze design.* [*Photo by Fred Kent*]

1. Prepare the bellows with an antique white (white with a little raw umber) on the front, and a rather dark, rosy-red (Concord red by Tole Finishes is a good color) on the outside stripe, handle A, and the back of the bellows.

2. Varnish the front; let it dry and then rub with fine steel wool.

3. Trace the design and transfer it to the bellows.

4. Dust the surface lightly with talcum powder and paint the heavily outlined units with black enamel or seal. When tacky, apply XX gold leaf and brush off the loose gold.

5. With black size, paint all the other units, including the stripe around the center design. When tacky, rub rich-gold bronze powder solidly on the stripe, and shade it on the other units so that a black edge remains.

6. Etch the gold leaf as shown; then paint stems, curleycues, and the lines and dots on the freehand-bronzed units. A stroke design is shown on the pattern next to the handle. Paint this design in black on the back of the bellows, around the hole.

7. Finish with handrubbing.

Tin box with country painting. [Courtesy of the Cooper-Hewitt Museum of Decorative Arts and Design, Smithsonian Institution]

PATTERN 18   *Tracing for design No. 1 of turtleback bellows.*

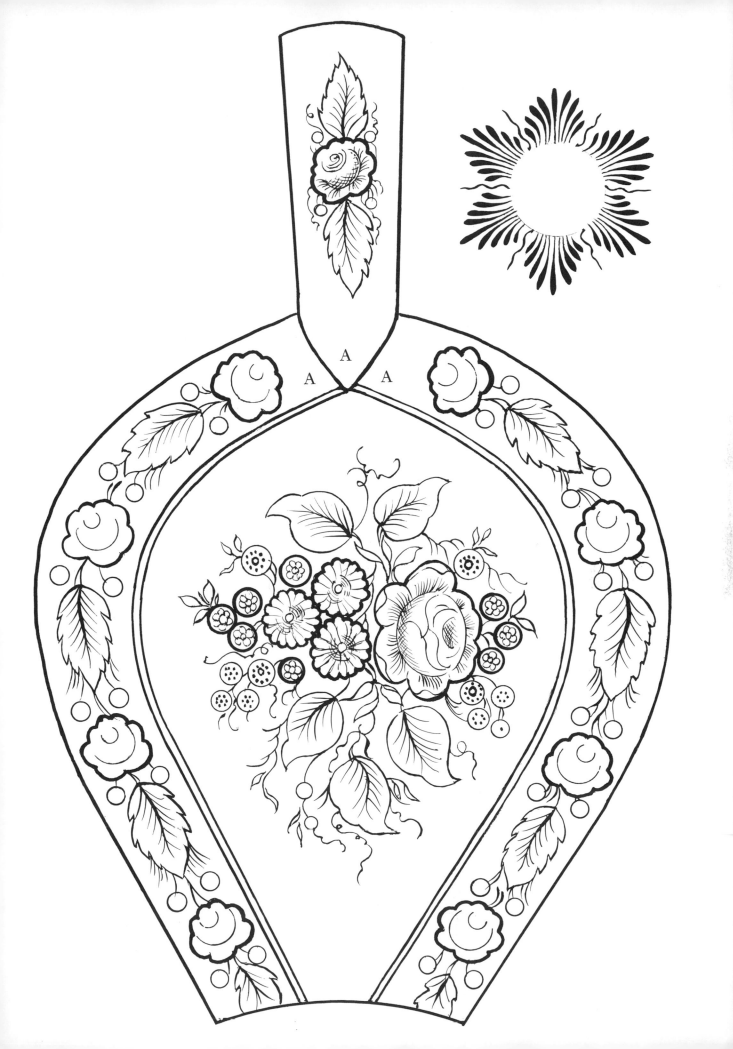

PATTERN 19

Turtleback bellows, design No. 2

1. Prepare the bellows with a warm-gray background (white with Vandyke brown).

2. Paint the two heavily outlined areas with black enamel or seal, and when tacky, apply lemon gold leaf.

3. Brush off the loose gold and paint all other units in black seal. When tacky, apply rich-gold bronze powder in the centers of all units marked A, blending off gradually to leave a black outline. On the other half of the gold-leafed leaf, blend the powder off toward both the center vein and the edge.

4. Cut an oval stencil for B and lay it on the area enclosed with a broken line; stencil in deep-gold powder, shading it. Cut some curved edges on linen, lay them along the broken lines on the outside petals of B, and stencil in silver powder. Stencil C in the same way, leaving sharp edges at the places indicated by the broken lines.

5. Apply silver powder to all the remaining unmarked units, shading from the center to the edges.

6. Paint the stripe in seal, and when tacky, rub on rich-gold powder.

7. Wash off all excess powder and etch the gold-leaf units as indicated.

8. Paint in black the stems, curleycues, and all the veins and fine lines on the bronzed units.

9. Finish with handrubbing.

PATTERN 19 *Tracing for design No. 2 of turtleback bellows (Figure 41).*

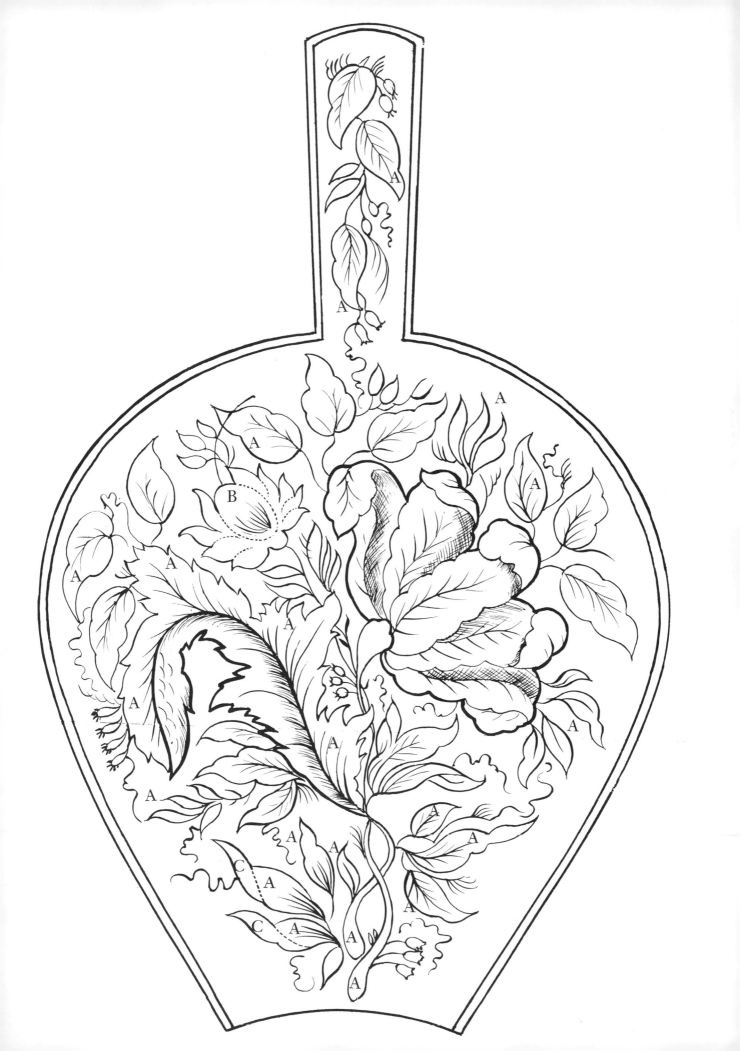

Pattern 20

Portfolio cover with mother-of-pearl (Figure 42)

1. Prepare the article with a black background and inlaid mother-of-pearl in the sections marked A (see Chapter IX). On a pattern, substitute palladium leaf with thin washes of red and blue to simulate the pearl.

2. Paint all the solid-black areas in a green that is slightly yellower than country green.

FIGURE 42 *Portfolio cover with Chippendale painting. Courtesy of Mrs. William Schwab, Gainesville, New York.* [*Photo by Fred Kent*]

PATTERN 20 *Tracing of design for portfolio cover (Figure 42).*

3. Paint flowers B in orange-red with a bit of burnt umber, and C flowers and buds in a medium-light gray-blue (white, Prussian blue, and raw umber).

4. Paint the other three flowers in semitransparent white.

5. When these base coats are dry, give the roses (one at a time) a wash of clear varnish; while still wet, float a wash of alizarin crimson with a little burnt umber over the top half of the flower and brush lightly at the edge to blend it into the clear varnish. The blending should be gradual so that the two lower petals are only slightly tinted.

6. Float a wash of thin raw umber over flower D; while still wet, paint the outlined circle in thin orange-red, and blend at the edges. Work a very light mauve tone (Prussian blue and alizarin crimson) around the flower just above the lower petals. This should be well blended, with the change of color so subtle that it is hardly noticeable.

7. Paint a wide stroke of thin alizarin crimson over the top three petals of red flower B that is to the left of flower D, and blend at the broken line. Add another stroke at the tip of the bottom petal. Paint thin alizarin crimson on the other B flower from the broken line *down* to the edges of the petals.

8. Paint a wash of Prussian blue (heavier than the red washes) on blue flower C (the one directly below flower D) from the broken line to flower D; on the other C flower, paint the same Prussian-blue wash from the broken lines to the edges of the petals. Paint a blue wash on the right side of each of buds C.

9. Within the outlines of the roses, paint semitransparent white strokes, making the upper small strokes more transparent and some of the larger ones a little less transparent.

10. On the leaves paint thin raw-umber strokes within the broken lines; paint the veins in black. On the red and blue flowers, the stamens are chrome yellow, medium.

11. The border stripe and corners are gold leaf. If you use this with the design, either apply it first, or wait until after the painted design has been varnished and allowed to dry for a week.

12. Finish the article with handrubbing.

Patterns 21a, 21b, and 21c

Chippendale tray 12½ by 15 inches (Figure 43)

1. Prepare the tray with a black background.
2. Trace the center design and transfer it to the tray.
3. Paint the heavily outlined areas A, B, and C (Pattern 21a) with yellow size, and when tacky, lay XX gold leaf. Brush off the loose gold.
4. Using a mixture of burnt sienna and burnt umber, paint the column on which bird B is perched. Disregard the overlapping flowers and leaves, but wipe any edges which cut through these units so that no ridges will show when they are painted over the column.
5. Paint thin burnt sienna on gold-leaf C and add a stroke of heavier burnt umber on the left.
6. Paint the following in semitransparent white: flowers D and E within the broken outlines; flowers I and G; the base coat for small flowers H; the long, outlined strokes in K, L, and M; the entire bunch of grapes; and flowers N. Be sure the wash on C is dry.
7. Paint morning glory J in a more opaque white than that used in Step 6.
8. Paint thin white on the birds' tails in long, wide strokes which feather off at the tips. Let the white strokes on bird B cover the gold leaf almost up to the wing.
9. Paint all curleycues, stems, and solid-black areas in a soft yellow green (country green with yellow added).
10. When these base coats are dry, paint the following overlays:

FIGURE 43 *Chippendale tray.* [*Photo by Charles Ferry*]

PATTERN 21a   *Tracing for center design of Chippendale tray (Figure 43).*

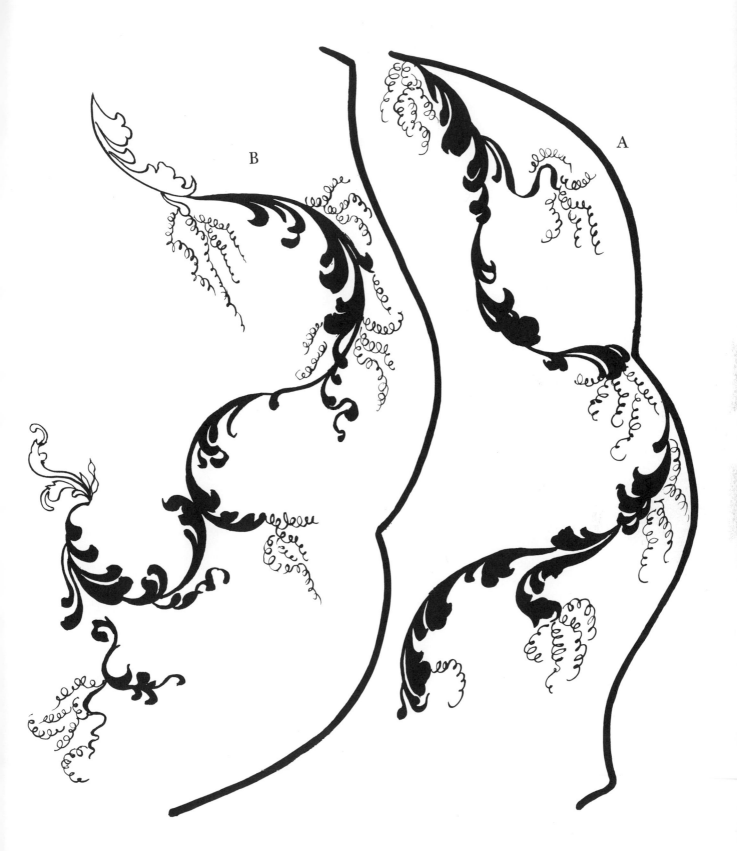

PATTERN 21b *Border-design tracing for right side of Chippendale tray (Figure 43).*

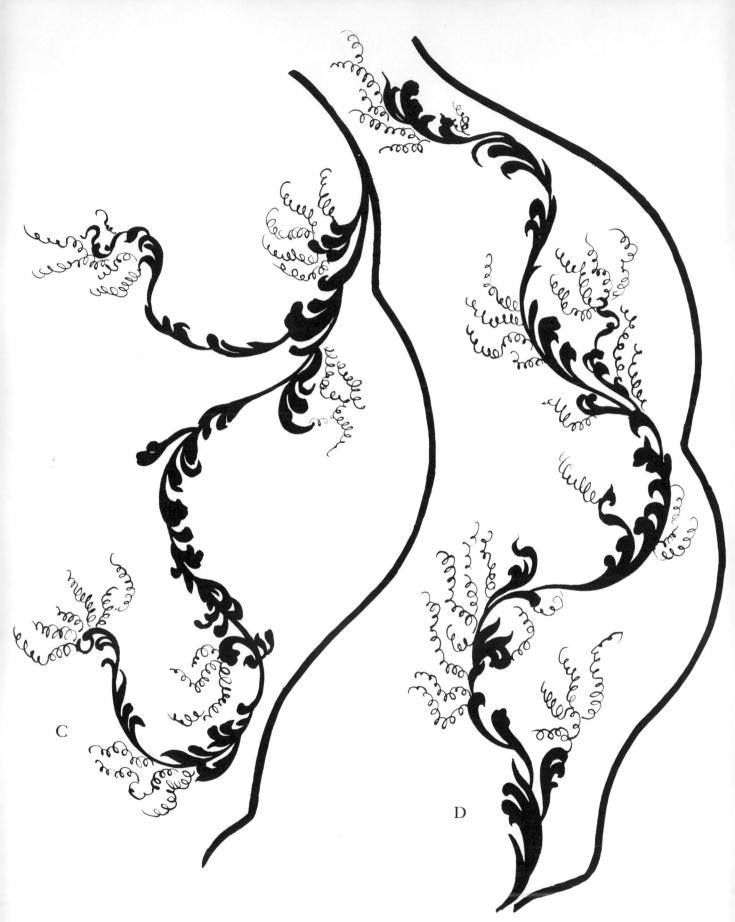

C

D

PATTERN 21C *Border-design tracing for left side of Chippendale tray (Figure 43).*

Bird A—In the shaded area on the body, Prussian-blue wash blending to yellow on the head and down to yellow to red (alizarin crimson and burnt umber) at the bottom of the wing. Paint slightly less transparent strokes on the tail, ending just inside the base coat. When these layers are dry, add black strokes on the wing and one white stroke (outlined). The two on the head are thin white. Add a few more heavier white strokes (outlined) on the tail and a black eye with a tiny circle of white inside.

Bird B—A thin wash of yellow green on the head and upper part of the body, blending to burnt umber and alizarin crimson on the breast. Paint the entire tail with alizarin crimson and burnt umber, and add a blended burnt-umber stroke on the top of the wing. Over the eye and just touching the wing (outlined), paint a large, thin, white stroke. When these layers are dry, paint deep Prussian-blue strokes on the wing (solid black), black lines on the wing, and a white stroke (outlined) which goes over the blue. Paint eye as on bird A, with burnt sienna strokes underneath.

Column—Overstrokes and lines are burnt umber.

Flower D—A thin wash of raw umber and transparent yellow over entire flower, just slightly heavier under the cup section. When dry, paint the transparent white petals. These strokes are outlined, and since some are complete strokes and others overlap, they will have to be done with a side-loaded brush. The solid-black strokes are painted in more opaque white after the petals have dried. The small shaded area in the center of the cup can be painted with two or three small, thin, burnt-sienna strokes.

Flowers E, F, and H—The outlined strokes are painted in thin white, and the solid-black strokes are heavy white accents. In the center of E are three or four thin yellow and burnt-sienna strokes. In the small flowers H the centers are burnt sienna with a yellow dot.

Flower G—Yellow dots, and when dry, a wash of alizarin crimson and burnt umber over the shaded area.

Flowers K, L, and M—Heavier white strokes on the solid-black areas and thin burnt-sienna strokes in the centers.

Flowers N—Heavy white strokes and yellow dots.

Grapes—A wash of transparent yellow with a speck of raw umber over the top of the bunch, blending to burnt umber and alizarin crimson in the shaded area. When dry, add semitransparent white strokes in the outlined areas, and opaque white where the strokes and dots are black.

Flower J—On the funnel a very thin wash of Prussian blue and raw umber. A thin blue wash on the petals around the white center, blending at the broken line. When dry, add deeper blue strokes (solid outlines) and thin white strokes (broken outlines). Add some thin burnt-sienna strokes, starting at the deep-blue curve out toward the broken line.

Flower I—Paint thin white strokes, as indicated by the broken lines. When dry, paint the small center black strokes in yellow. When these are dry, add thin burnt umber and alizarin strokes within the solid outlines. All these overstrokes should be kept thin and not too clearly delineated, as the flower should sink into the background.

Leaves—Paint the outlined strokes in raw umber. The solid-white strokes are pale yellow (chrome yellow, medium; burnt umber, and a little white).

11. When the entire center design is finished and thoroughly dry, clean off spots, and varnish; when tacky, brush a little statuary bronze powder at P.

12. Allow to dry for a week. Rub with steel wool No. 0000. Then trace the border design (Patterns 21b and 21c) and transfer to the tray. From Pattern 21b, place A in the upper right portion, and B in the lower right; from Pattern 21c, place C in the upper left portion and D in the lower left.

13. Dust a thin layer of talcum powder on the border, paint the design in yellow size, and when it is tacky, lay XX gold leaf. The curleycues can be done with a pen. Stripe the edge with deep-gold powder on tacky enamel.

14. Finish with handrubbing.

PATTERN 22

Lace-edge tray, 8¼ inches in diameter (Figure 44)

1. Prepare the tray with a black background.
2. Trace the design and transfer to the tray.
3. Dust the border with talcum powder and paint the design in yellow size. When tacky, apply XX gold leaf.
4. Brush off the loose gold and paint the buds within the solid outline and those over the black strokes in orange-red with a little burnt umber and white.
5. When dry, float a wash of alizarin crimson and burnt umber over the buds making the wash deeper at the base.

FIGURE 44 *Small lace-edge tray.* [*Photo by Fred Kent*]

PATTERN 22   *Tracing for design of small lace-edge tray (Figure 44)*.

6. When this is dry, mix white with a speck of orange-red and some wax medium (Chapter VII), and paint a thin veil over the buds, keeping the mixture thinner on the shaded sides. Add some heavier white strokes on the light sides. Paint a stroke of thin orange-red at the base of the shaded areas.

7. Paint the small flowers, using the wax medium. The white petals are white and the shaded petals are a medium blue toned down with a little raw umber. Center strokes are white.

8. The leaves are a blue-green and can be painted like the sample in Figure 23. The white and yellow-ochre overstrokes are indicated by a white outline. The strokes on the edges and tips are the same color. Paint all other solid-black areas in a similar green, with overstrokes of the light yellow.

9. The groups of short fine lines are done in orange-red. The painted border consists of green strokes and red dots.

10. When the painting is dry (it will require a longer period than usual because of the wax medium), finish with handrubbing.

Tin box with country painting. [*Courtesy of the* Cooper-Hewitt Museum of Decorative Arts and Design, Smithsonian Institution]

PATTERN 23

Stenciled glass, 8 by 10 inches, for shelf clock

1. Trace the pattern on linen and cut out.
2. Varnish the glass and stencil the design in silver powder, following the directions given in Chapter XI.
3. Rub smudges of rich-gold powder on the head and wing of the bird, and copper or fire powder on the breast.
4. When dry, wash and back up with asphaltum around the border and Prussian blue within the broken lines and side bars.

Round lace-edge tray.

PATTERN 23 *Stenciled glass design for shelf clock.*

PATTERN 24

Mirror frame, 20 by 24 inches, with decorated glass panels (Figure 45)

1. Have a wooden mirror frame made like A; a cross section of one side is shown by B. The frame can be any size. I have decorated smaller and much larger ones.

2. Have eight glass panels cut—four to fit into C and four to fit into D. The paint will take up some of the space, so don't have the fit too tight.

3. Paint all the shaded areas in B (the inside and outside edges and raised molding) with sanding primer, prepared gesso, or flat-white paint. Give them two or three coats and sand until very smooth. Paint with white shellac, and when dry, sand smooth.

FIGURE 45 *Mirror frame with decorated glass panels.* [*Photo by Fred Kent*]

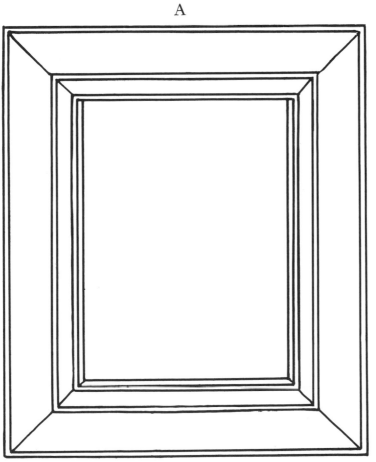

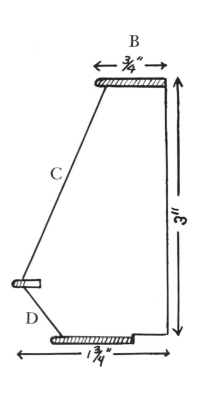

PATTERN 24   Below: *Wooden mirror frame, with cross section of one side.*
Above: *Tracing for design on glass panels in mirror frame (Figure 45).*

A

B

¾″

C

3″

D

1¾″

4. Paint varnish or gold size on these areas, and when tacky, lay XX gold leaf. Brush off the loose gold.

5. Trace the border design shown, or any other suitable border design, repeating the units until there are enough to fill the glass panel. Lay the tracing under the glass panel; then apply gold leaf and etch it, back it up, and clean it, according to the directions given in Chapter XI. Follow the same procedure for the other panels.

6. When all the excess gold has been cleaned off, the panels can be backed with palladium leaf, as is the one illustrated; or they can be painted with semigloss white paint. The palladium leaf, if used, would be laid the same way as the gold leaf; it requires more work than the paint but is no more effective.

7. Varnish the backs of the panels and let dry for at least a week.

8. The next step is to attach the glass panels to the wooden frame with an adhesive. As with paints and varnishes, the ingredients in adhesives have been changing rapidly and new products are constantly appearing on the market. Some spray adhesives are satisfactory, as are some of the ones used for laying tile; but you must be sure that the one you select will not adversely affect paint or varnish. For this reason, it would be wise to test the adhesive on a piece of painted glass before using it to attach the panels to the frame.

9. From the back, lay the mirror (cut to the proper size) into the frame. Place a piece of cardboard over it and tack in place. Cut a piece of brown paper the same size as the back of the frame. Apply rubber cement to the edges of both the frame and the paper, and press the paper onto the frame, pulling it taut. Insert screw eyes on both sides of the frame a few inches from the top. Attach picture wire, and the mirror is ready to hang.

PATTERN 25

Scene painted on mirror glass (Figure 46)

1. Have a piece of glass cut 8 by 10 inches.
2. Trace the design, reverse the tracing, and lay it under the glass. Tape together.
3. Apply XX gold leaf on the border over the flowers, as described in Chapter XI. Etch the center oval and lines, and back up with black seal.
4. When dry, remove the excess gold; then paint the irregular ovals over the flowers in burnt umber.
5. With a ruling pen and flat-black paint, draw the border line.
6. Mix some burnt sienna with a little burnt umber, and using a stencil brush, stipple the dots on either side of the gold-leaf units—rather heavily near the center, and less heavily and farther apart nearer the corners. Mix a grayed yellow-green (chrome yellow, medium; raw umber; and a little Prussian blue) and with a clean stencil brush, stipple in the same area so that the colors are juxtaposed.
7. When dry, paint the background on the border in white. If it needs toning, add a little raw umber.
8. Paint the scene in four steps, with the colors indicated below. Let each color dry before applying the next layer. Blend colors between broken lines.

FIGURE 46 *Scene for a mirror achieved by reverse glass-painting. [Photo by Charles Ferry]*

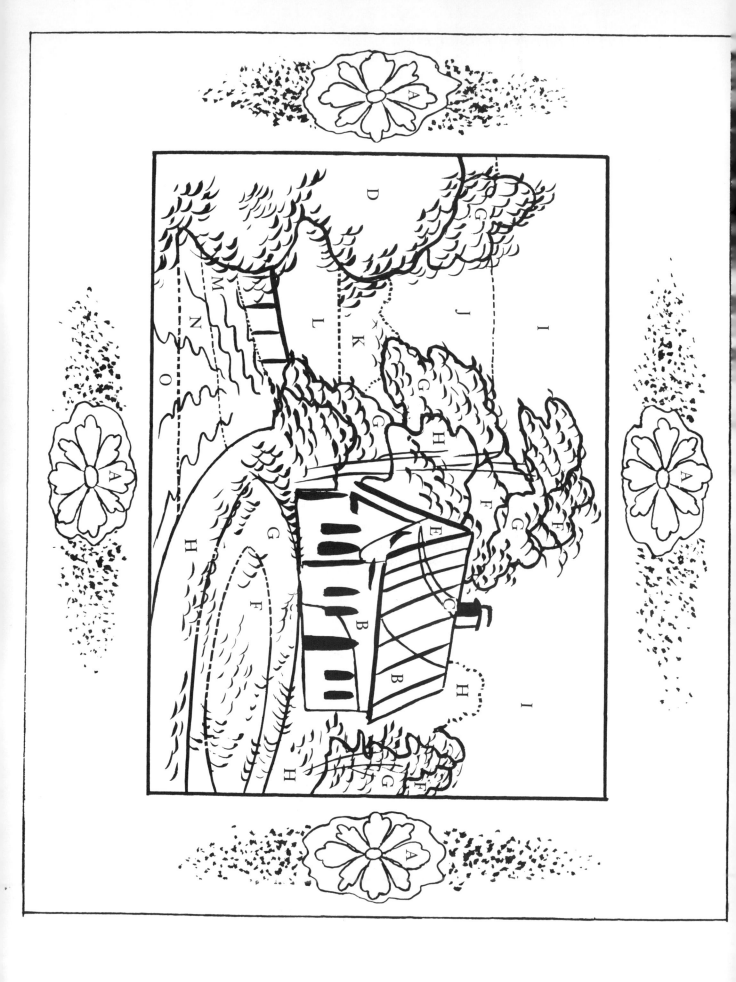

ɪ. For all black strokes; for the wiggly lines on the road; and for the heavy lines outlining the house, windows, door, branches and the fence, use raw umber (with black, if the raw umber is not deep enough) or burnt umber. Area B, stroke C, and the chimney are in burnt umber.

ɪɪ. Rock D in burnt umber, darker around the edges. Roof in red, lighter and grayer at upper left corner and deeper just below stroke C. Area E in white with raw umber. Just below this stroke, pale yellow blending into white to finish the end of the house. Front of house in burnt umber.

ɪɪɪ. Trees and grass in three shades of green: sections F in yellow-green (chrome yellow and raw umber); sections G in medium green (the same mixture as for F, with a little Prussian blue added); sections H in dark umbery green (again, the same mixture; but this time add a little more blue and much more raw umber).

ɪv. Section I in light gray-blue (white, a little blue, raw umber, and just a speck of alizarin crimson if it seems too greenish). Section J in pale yellow (white; very little chrome yellow, medium; and raw umber). Section K in raw umber with a speck of Prussian blue. Section L same as I. Section M same as J, with the addition of a bit more yellow. Section N in burnt sienna. Section O in burnt umber. At the broken line between I and J, and those between M, N, and O, blend the colors so that no line of demarcation is visible. At other broken lines, blend only enough to leave a soft outline.

PATTERN 25   *Tracing of reverse glass-painting of scene for a mirror (Figure 46).*

PATTERN 26

Mirror glass, 7 by 9 inches. Basket of fruit (Figure 47)

1. Trace the design, reverse it, and tape the 7 by 9 inch glass over it.

2. Paint the border, using the same steps listed for Pattern 25. The only difference is that the gold-leaf shells are etched more extensively and the stippled color is a little heavier and brighter.

3. Paint the center design in four steps, using the colors indicated below. Let the paint used in each step dry thoroughly before going on to the next step, and blend colors that are separated by a broken line.

    I. All solid outlines and black strokes in burnt umber. After the burnt-umber lines have set up, do the dots in the grapes and the outlined strokes on the basket in white.

    II. H in fairly bright green, blending into chrome yellow and raw umber on the other sides of the leaves. B in alizarin crimson with a speck of Prussian blue, blending into C with a little more blue and burnt umber added. Let B blend off to nothing at the broken line next to A. For E use red-violet (alizarin crimson and blue), blending at D to nothing. F in rather deep burnt umber with a touch of white.

FIGURE 47   *Reverse glass-painting of a basket of fruit for a mirror. Courtesy of Mrs. Ira*   *Robinson, Barre, Vermont. [Photo by Charles Ferry]*

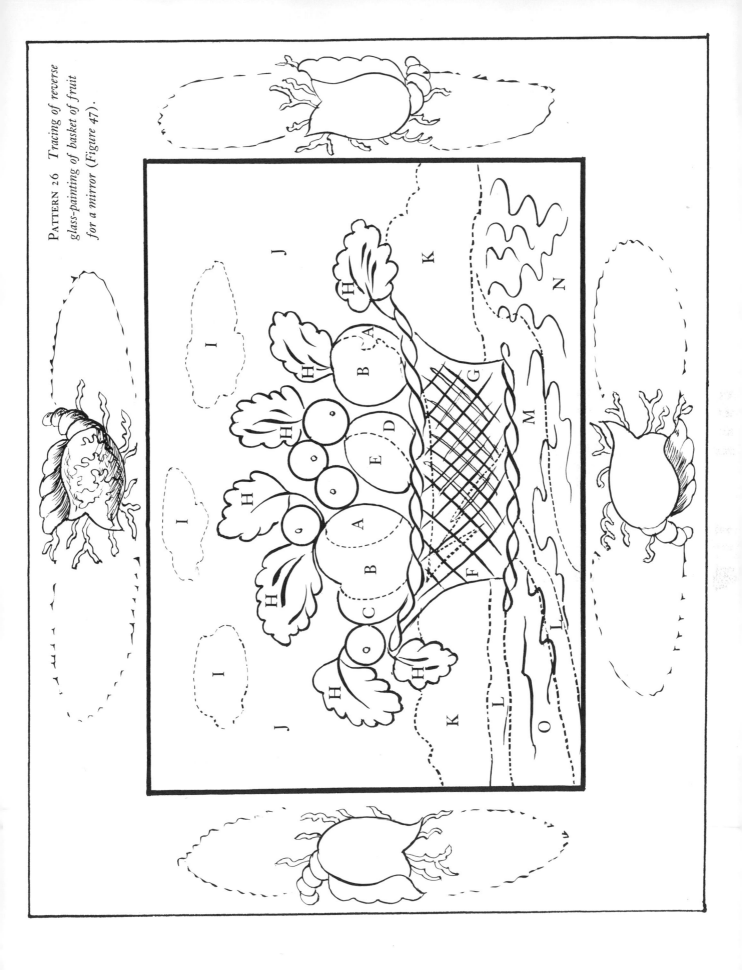

III. Grapes in two shades of gray-blue, keeping the deeper shade to the bottom right. Paint A in white with a bit of raw umber, extending the color over B and C also. Basket G in straw color (yellow ochre and raw umber) continuing over F. Mix a little orange-red in oil, blend it into the straw-color mixture, and with your finger, push a little into the right side of the basket. The change from the straw color should be scarcely noticeable.

IV. J in light gray-blue (white, blue, and raw umber). While J is still wet, add a little alizarin crimson to the blue mixture and with the finger, push some of this color into the background at I, blending out into J. Here, too, the color change should be barely visible. K in deep gray-blue (Prussian blue, black, and a little white). N in yellow and burnt umber; add some blue to this same mixture for M, and more blue and more raw umber for L. Work in some black at O to suggest a shadow. The colors on the left covering K, L, O, and M are very close in value.

PATTERN 27

Tinsel picture (Figure 48)

1. Trace the pattern and place it in reverse under a piece of glass 8 by 10 inches that has been treated as described in Chapter XI. Tape in place.

2. Draw the outlines and shading lines, and paint a white background, again following the directions given in Chapter XI.

3. Paint thinly with transparent colors, adding deeper color in the shadow areas. A is alizarin crimson with a little transparent yellow; the base of the poppy is green. B is transparent yellow with a bit of burnt umber in the shadows; the five crescents are green, and the center is burnt umber and alizarin crimson. C is purple, blending to yellow at B. The bird, D, is blue, with the deeper tone on the breast, wing tips, and tail. E is white, blending to green at the yellow center; the seven outlined strokes are purple. Leaves and stems are green. Vary the mixtures so that some are more yellow and some more blue. In the shadow areas add burnt umber to the yellow-greens, and raw umber to the blue-greens.

4. When the paint is dry, back the glass with crumpled foil, and frame.

FIGURE 48 *Crumpled foil backing a reverse glass-painting produces a tinsel picture.* [*Photo by Charles Ferry*]

231]

PATTERN 27   *Tracing of design for a tinsel picture (Figure 48).*

Epilogue

WHAT NEXT? Now that you have worked with some of the Early American decorating techniques you may want to explore this new world of art expression further. Your immediate need after gaining some mastery of the painting methods will be to acquire more designs to use on various types of articles. The best sources are experienced teachers who have built up their pattern collections from originals or copies made by other teachers. You may be able to copy some originals, too. Family or friends sometimes discover unexpected treasures in their attics when they become aware of your new interest. Some pattern books are available which are helpful for the simpler designs.

As you become more skilled in handling the various techniques you may find that your work is marketable. Collectors and antique dealers often have a need for experienced decorators to restore or redecorate tinware or furniture. Gift and craft shops are always looking for new items. The teaching field is wide open in many parts of the country.

Association with other craftsmen is always inspiring. The Historical Society of Early American Decoration is a guild of decorators which was formed by students of Esther Stevens Brazer to carry on her research and to increase interest in the preservation of decorated antiques. Mrs. Brazer, who was teaching at about the same time as my own instructor, Mr. Crowell, did much to revive the early craft through her articles and book. Her collection of originals is on display in Cooperstown, New York, and members of the society are permitted to record the decorations as well as to make copies of her patterns. Membership in the organization is conditional upon the acceptance of two examples of the applicant's work and is well worth the effort involved.

The possibilities in the field of decorative painting are almost infinite, and your interests may develop in any one of the many aspects of the craft—transforming a piece of rusty tin into a thing of beauty, finding new ideas for creating your own designs, or searching out rare examples of early decoration. In any case, I hope you will find the whole experience, as I did, an exciting one.

APPENDIX

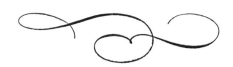

Supplies and Equipment

THE FOLLOWING SUPPLIES will eventually be needed if the reader chooses to work in *all* the decorating techniques described in this book. However, if he prefers to concentrate on only one or two techniques, then, of course, only some of the listed items will be necessary. Many of the items are probably part of household equipment already.

To help the beginning craftsman, some of the supplies which might be unfamiliar have been described in each chapter.

Some of the other materials used by decorators are also mentioned in the book. When you become more involved in this craft you may want to experiment with these materials and others that come to your attention.

BASIC LIST

Art & Sign Brushes (or similar brushes from other companies)
    ¾ inch square-tipped quills, Series 484, Nos. 1, 2, 3, 5
    Short-pointed quills, Series 472, Nos. 2, 4
    Long-pointed quills, Series 480, Nos. 1, 2
    Striping quill, Series 489, No. 1
    Scrollers, Series 831, Nos. 1, 2
    Finepoint, Series 9, No. 2
    The Spotter, Series 12, or Everpoint, Series 8, Nos. 4, 5, 6
    Ox-hair stroke, Series 221, ⅜ inch and ⅞ inch
    Ox-hair signwriters (for varnishing), Series 224, 1 inch
    Bright's red sable, Series 824, Nos. 1, 3, 8
    Soft, flat, camel- or squirrel-hair brush (for gold leaf)

Tube Paints (in japan)
    Striping white
    Chrome yellow, medium
    Medium orange (King Cole) or Signcraft red (Ronan) in can

Appendix

Tube Paints (artists' oil colors)
Cadmium red, light
Alizarin crimson
Prussian blue
Yellow lake or Indian yellow
Yellow ochre
Raw umber
Burnt umber
Burnt sienna

Paints and Varnishes (in cans)
Gloss varnish (see Chapters I and X for description)
Semigloss varnish
Dark-oak varnish stain
Black asphaltum or asphaltum varnish
Black enamel or black seal
Yellow enamel
Flat-black paint
Flat white (enamel undercoat)

Tools
Stylus; or lead pencil, No. 8H
White pencil
Compass
Etching needles, single and triple (for gold leaf)
Palette knife
Crow-quill pen or tracing pen
Black drawing ink (India)
X-acto knife, No. 11 or No. 16 blade
Stencil scissors
Rubber dam punch
Leather punch
Carborundum (for sharpening stencil knife)
Charcoal stumps
Ruler
Sharp shears

Abrasives and Polishing Materials
Wet-or-dry sandpaper, Nos. 400, 600
Fine garnet sandpaper
Steel wool, No. 0000
Rottenstone
Powdered pumice, 4F
Lava soap
Baby oil, crude oil, or paraffin oil
Butcher's bowling-alley wax
Soft flannel cloths

Paper and Cardboard
    Palette paper or paper palette
    Tracing paper
    Frosted acetate (Supersee), No. 3 (.003 inch)
    Clear acetate, No. 3 (.003 inch)
    Graphite paper (transfer)
    Architects' linen
    Newsprint (for practice)
    Black paper
    Wax paper
    Black cardboard
    White or gray cardboard (for mounting)

Miscellaneous
    Turpentine (gum)
    Energine or cleaning fluid
    Lard oil or Vaseline hair tonic
    Lithopone powder (for transfer paper)
    Talcum powder
    Silk velvet or chamois
    Nylon stockings
    Paint rags
    Tack rags
    Book of gold leaf
    Quickie hand cleaner
    Masking tape
    Scotch transparent tape
    Bronze lining powders (for stenciling)—aluminum or silver, rich gold, deep gold, fire
    Bohemian Guild Master Medium (for lace-edge painting)
    Piece of glass (about 8 by 10 inches) taped on edges
    Bottle caps or other containers

ADDITIONAL SUPPLIES FOR SPECIFIC TECHNIQUES

Stenciling on velvet (Chapter III)
    White cotton velvet
    Contact paper
    Lightweight wool; or stencil brushes, Series 608, Nos. 0–3
    Stencil paper

Stenciling on walls (Chapter III)
    Stencil brushes, Series 608, Nos. 4–6; or lightweight wool or flannel

Appendix

Laying gold leaf on irregular surfaces (*Chapter V*)
 Gilder's tip
 Gilder's cushion
 Slow oil size (if object is for outdoor use)

Restoring or stripping antique tin or wood (*Chapter VIII*)
 Denatured alcohol   Rust-i-cide
 Acetone   Coarse sandpaper and steel wool
 Paint remover   White shellac

Smoked backgrounds (*Chapter VIII*)
 Candle

Bronzed backgrounds (*Chapter VIII*)
 Piece of mouton or otter fur, or lamb's wool
 Large, round, camel- or squirrel-hair brush

Tortoise-shell background (*Chapter VIII*)
 Palladium leaf

Rosewood graining (*Chapter VIII*)
 Venetian red in japan   Old bristle brush or newspapers

Putty graining (*Chapter VIII*)
 Cider vinegar   Putty
 Maple syrup   Paper towels
 Dry pigments

Mother-of-pearl inlay (*Chapter IX*)
 Sheets of mother-of-pearl
 Manicure scissors
 White shellac and shellac thinner (for cleaning the brush)

Reverse glass painting (*Chapter XI*)
 Gelatin capsules, No. oo, or powdered gelatin
 Ruling pen
 Japan drier
 Stencil brush, Series 608, No. 3; or a piece of sponge
 Aluminum foil (for tinsel pictures)

Suppliers

Art and Decorating Supplies
 Arthur Brown and Bros., Inc.
  2 West 46th Street, New York, New York

Brenner's Paint Shop (Bohemian Guild Master Medium)
  8 Samoset Street, Plymouth, Massachusetts 02360
Carson & Ellis, Inc.
  1153 Warwick Avenue, Warwick, Rhode Island
Crafts Mfg. Co. (King Cole japan paints)
  Massachusetts Avenue, Lunenburg, Massachusetts
A. & A. J. Hutcheon, Inc.
  92 Pleasant Street, Claremont, New Hampshire
Keeler's Paint Works, Inc. (Fashion Design Quills)
  40 Green St., New London, Connecticut 06321

Bronze Powders (wholesale)
  Baer Brothers Bronze Powder Co.
    Division of O. A. Both Corp., Ashland, Massachusetts
  B. F. Drakenfeld & Co., Inc.
    45–47 Park Place, New York, New York
  Leo Uhlfelder Co.
    159 West 25th Street, New York, New York 10001

Brushes
  Art & Sign Brush Mfg. Corp. (wholesale)
    36–32 34th Street, Long Island City, New York 11106
  Mariette Paine Slayton (retail)
    R. F. D. 2, Montpelier, Vermont 05602

Cardboard and Paper
  Hampden Glazed Paper and Card Co. (Plasti-Sheen Cover)
    Holyoke, Massachusetts 01040
  Hazen Paper Co. (Hazenkote, a black paper)
    Holyoke, Massachusetts 01040
  Golden Eagle Studio (tracing paper, acetate, architects' linen)
    P. O. Box 94, North Chelmsford, Massachusetts 01863
  Major Services (acetates)
    1740 West Columbia Avenue, Chicago, Illinois
  C. M. Rice (black cardboard)
    Concord, New Hampshire
  Rourke-Eno Paper Co. (black cardboard, glossy and dull)
    Hartford, Connecticut
  Stanford Ink Co. (stencil paper)
    Bellwood, Illinois

Gold Leaf (wholesale)
  Hastings and Co.
    43 West 16th Street, New York, New York 10011
  M. Swift and Sons, Inc.
    10 Love Lane, Hartford, Connecticut

Appendix

Reproductions (wood and tin)

Cohasset Colonials (wood reproductions, knocked down)
    6 Ship Street, Cohasset, Massachusetts 02025
Colonial Handcraft Trays
    New Market, Virginia 22844
Chester P. Galleher (cut corner or coffin trays)
    105 Puritan Road, Rosslyn Farms, Carnegie, Pennsylvania 15106
Hitchcock Chair Co.
    Riverton, Connecticut
Dorothy Hutchings (tin)
    122 Andrews Road, De Witt, New York 13214

Miscellaneous

S. B. Albertis (Saral transfer paper)
    5 Tudor City Place, New York, New York 10017
Art Enterprises (mother-of-pearl)
    1578 West Lewis Street, San Diego, California 92103
H. Behlen and Bros., Inc. (japan paints and gold size)
    10 Christopher Street, New York, New York
Mrs. Robert Bliss (sells stencil scissors)
    Upper Terrace Street, Montpelier, Vermont 05602
Bohemian Guild Products (Master Medium)
    Paul Larkin, 323 Waltham Street, West Newton, Massachusetts 02165
Gina Martin (patterns for wall stenciling)
    359 Avery Street, Wapping, Connecticut 06074
Patricia Nimocks (mother-of-pearl)
    P. O. Box 7187, Louisville, Kentucky 40207
Shopsin Paper Co. (contact paper)
    92 Vandam Street, New York, New York 10013
J. S. Staedtler, Inc. (white pencils)
    Box 86, Montville, New Jersey
Stoddards (stencil scissors, Nos. 93–9CM)
    50 Temple Place, Boston, Massachusetts
S. Steinhauer & Sons (graphite paper)
    321 DeKalb Avenue, Brooklyn, New York 11205

BIBLIOGRAPHY

BOOKS

BRAZER, Esther Stevens, *Early American Decoration*. Springfield, Mass.: Pond-Ekberg Co., 1940.

CHRISTIANSEN, Erwin O., *The Index of American Design*. New York: Macmillan Co., 1950.

CLARK, Mary Jane, *17th Century to the Early 20th Century*. Rutland, Vt. and Tokyo, Japan: Charles E. Tuttle Co., Historical Society of Early American Decoration, 1971.

COFFIN, Margaret, *The History and Folklore of American Country Tinware. (1700–1900)*. Camden, N. J.: Thomas Nelson & Sons, 1968.

CRAMER, Edith, *Handbook of Early American Decoration*. Boston: Charles T. Branford Co., 1951.

DEVOE, Shirley Spaulding, *The Tinsmiths of Connecticut*. Middletown, Conn.: Wesleyan University Press, 1968.

GOULD, Mary Earle, *Antique Tin & Toleware: Its History and Romance*. Rutland, Vt.: Charles E. Tuttle Co., 1958.

HALL, Peg, *Early American Decorating Patterns*. New York: M. Barrows and Co., Inc., 1951.

HALLETT, Charles, *Furniture Decoration Made Easy*. Boston: Charles T. Branford Co., 1952.

JOHN, W. D. *Pontypool and Usk Japanned Ware*. Newport, England: Ceramic Book Co., 1953.

LEA, Zilla Rider, ed., *The Ornamented Chair: Its Development in America*. Rutland, Vt.: Charles E. Tuttle Co., 1960.

———, *The Ornamented Tray 1720–1920*. Rutland, Vt.: Charles E. Tuttle Co., 1970.

LITTLE, Nina Fletcher, *American Decorative Wall Painting*. New York: Studio Publications, 1952.

———, *Country Art in New England 1790–1840*. Sturbridge, Mass.: Old Sturbridge Village, 1960.

McCLINTON, Katharine Morrison, *A Handbook of Popular Antiques*. New York: Random House, 1945.

MURRAY, Maria D., *The Art of Tray Painting*. New York: Bramhall House, 1954.

SABINE, Ellen S., *Early American Decorative Patterns*. Princeton, N. J.: D. Van Nostrand Co., Inc., 1958.

SAYER, Robert, *The Ladies' Amusement or the Whole Art of Japanning Made Easy* (facsimile of 1762 edition by W. D. John, ed.). Newport, England: Ceramic Book Co., 1959.

Bibliography

WARING, Janet, *Early American Stencils on Walls and Furniture*. Watkins Glen, N. Y.: Century House, 1937.

WILSON, Nadine Cox, *A Guide to Decoration in the Early American Manner*. Rutland, Vt.: Charles E. Tuttle Co., 1965.

PERIODICALS AND PAMPHLETS

COFFIN, Margaret Mattison, "Dictionary of American Painted Furniture," *Woman's Day*, July 1966.

———, Little, Nina Fletcher "Dictionary of American Painted Tinware," *Woman's Day*, July 1964.

"THE DECORATOR"—a semiannual publication of the Historical Society of Early American Decoration (available from Miss Jean Wylie, 40 Fitch Avenue, Noroton Heights, Conn.).

POOLE, Earl L., "Reverse Glass Painting," Bulletin 18, Reading Public Museum and Art Gallery, 500 Museum Road, Reading, Pa.

INDEX

Acetate, frosted, 17
Antiquing, 109–111
Architects' linen, 25
Asphaltum, 92

Backgrounds
  bronzed, 94
  opaque, 91–92
  problems, 125–126
  smoked, 93–94
  tortoise-shell, 94–95
  transparent, 92–93
Bands, white and gold, 98–100,
  101, 118
Bellows patterns, 203–204, 206
Black cardboard and paper, 6
Blooming, 32
Bobs, 51
Box patterns, 142, 152, 200, 202
Bronze powders, 26–27
  backgrounds, 94
  bands, 100
  fineness, 126–127
  striping, 104
Brushes, 136–137
  background painting, 88
  bright's brush, 4
  cleaning, 4
  cost, 3
  Fashion Design Quill, 4
  Finepoint, 4
  for freehand bronze, 48
  gilder's tip, 57
  for lace-edge painting, 80
  liner, 4
  long-pointed quill, 4–5
  poly, 25
  scroller, 4
  shaping, 4
  spotter, 65
  square-tipped quill, 7
  stencil, 27
  storage, 4, 106
  striping, 97–98
  varnishing, 25, 106
Brush strokes, basic, 7–10

Chair patterns, 174, 178–179
Chamois, 25

Chippendale painting, 64–65
  colors, 70
  exercises, 68, 70
  flowers, 65–67, 72–76
  "indirect method," 65
  materials, 65
  method, 65–68, 70
  problems, 129
Chippendale trays, 24, 211, 215–
  216
Coffin trays, 24, 138
Colors, 137
  artists' oils, 4–5
  blending, 20
  chart, 16
  Chippendale painting, 70
  country painting, 5
  floating, 19–20, 32–34, 126
  hue, 14–16
  intensity, 14–16
  japan, 5
  matching, 15–16
  opaque, 16
  problems, 126
  semitransparent, 16
  striping, 102
  transparent, 16
  value, 14–16
  velvet stencils, 40–41
  wall stencils, 44
  wheel, 14–15
  wood, 91–93
Contact paper, 26
Country painting, 3
  base coats, 10–13
  Chippendale painting, 65
  colors, 5
  dots, 10
  materials, 4–6, 17
  pattern reproduction, 20–21
  problems, 125–126
  strokes, 7–10, 17–19
  techniques, 19–22
Crow-quill pen, 17
Crude oil, 106
Curleycues, 18, 122–123

Design application, 97–98, 130–
  131

Easels, 17
Etchers and etching, 55, 57, 60–
  61, 128–132

Finishes and finishing, 106–107,
  109
  alcohol-proof, 111
  antiquing, 109–111
  handrubbing, 109
  materials, 105–106
  outdoor, 105, 111
  powders, 106
  problems, 131
  See also Varnishes and var-
    nishing
Framing, 35, 124
Freehand bronze, 47
  materials, 48, 51–52
  painting, 48
  problems, 127–128
  shaded units, 48, 49, 51
  solid units, 48
French curves, 113

Gelatin, 113, 116
Gilding, 53, 57
Glass and glass painting, 112–
  113, 119–121
  fragments, 113
  gold leaf on, 115–119, 121–122
  materials, 113
  patterns, 220, 222, 224–225,
    227–228, 230, 231
  problems, 132
  repairing, 121–122
  stenciling, 113–115
  tinsel painting, 122–124, 132
Gold leaf, 53
  application, 58
  bands, 100, 101, 118
  Chippendale painting, 64
  etching, 57, 60
  on glass, 115–119, 121–122
  on irregular surfaces, 62–63
  materials, 55, 57
  matte gold, 62–63
  painting, 57–58
  problems, 128, 132
  repairing, 60
  shading, 61

Gold leaf—*Continued*
  sizing, 54–55
  squiggles, 61–62
  stenciling, 59–60
  stormont, 61–62
  striping, 104
Gothic tray, 64
Graining, 86, 95–96
Graphite paper, 97

Handrubbing, 109
Historical Society of Early
  American Decoration,
  233
Hitchcock chair, 24, 86

Japan drier, 113
Japanned ware, 47

Lace-edge painting, 77
  flowers, 80–82
  leaves, 82
  materials, 79
  patterns, 217, 219
  problems, 129
  strokes, 80
Litharge, 118
Lithopone powder, 88

Magnifying glasses, 24
Master Medium, 77, 79
Mica, 122
Mirror patterns, 222, 224, 225,
  227, 228, 230
Mother-of-pearl, 101–102

Oriental painting, 122
Overstrokes, 18–19

Palette knife, 16
Palettes, 6, 26
Palladium leaf, 53, 94–95
Paper
  black, 6
  stencil, 25
  tracing, 17
  transfer, 97
Paraffin oil, 91, 106
Patterns
  copying, 20–21
  mounting, 22
  originals, 135
  storing, 22
  See also specific articles and
    techniques
Pearl painting, 122
Pie Crust tray, 64
Portfolio cover patterns, 208,
  210
Primers, 86

Pumice stone, 106
Punches, 24

Queen Anne tray, 64

Rags, 6, 106
Rocker patterns, 168, 171
Rottenstone, 98, 106
Ruling pen, 113

Sandpaper, 87
Sandwich Gothic trays, 64
Scroller, 126
Shading, 65–67
Silver leaf, 53, 94–95
Sizes, 54–55, 57, 116
Squiggles, 17, 61–62, 101
Stand oil, 55
Stems and veins, 17
Stencils and stenciling, 23–24
  application, 29–31
  bronze-powder, 23–24, 28
  brush, 32
  cleaning, 29, 42
  cutting, 27–29
  enlarging a design, 36
  floating colors, 32–34
  foliage, 34
  on glass, 113–115
  gold leaf, 59–60
  materials, 24–27
  mending, 29
  multicolor, 32
  negative, 32
  problems, 126–127
  silhouettes, 32
  on tin, 27
  tracing, 27
  on velvet, *see* Velvet painting
  wall, 42–46; patterns, 192, 199
  on wood, 27
Stormont, 61–62
Striping, 89–90, 102–104, 130–
  131
Stumps, 51
Supersee, 17

Tack rag, 106
Tea caddy pattern, 150
Template, 24
Theorem painting, *see* Velvet
  painting
Tin
  antique, 86, 88
  new, 91
  problems, 130
  restoration, 88
  stripping, 89–90
Tinsel painting, 122–124, 132
  pattern, 231

Toleware, 3
Tracing, 100–101
Tracing paper, 17
Tracing pen, 17
Transfer paper, 97
"Tray flower," 65
Trays
  bands, 98, 100
  Chippendale, 64
  coffin, 98
  finishes, 85
  freehand bronze, 47
  gold leaf, 59–60
  lace-edge, 77, 94
  octagonal, 104
  position for painting, 98
  patterns, 138, 140, 154, 157,
    158, 162–164, 167, 180, 185,
    211, 215, 215–217, 219
  stenciling, 24
  striping, 103
  varnishing, 30
Trunk patterns, 144, 146, 149

Varnishes and varnishing, 106–
  107, 109
  brands recommended, 5
  brush, 25, 106
  colorless, 105
  gloss, 105
  mastic, 55
  mixing, 16
  outdoor, 105, 111
  problems, 131
  semigloss, 105
  storage, 5
Velvet painting, 25, 35
  application, 40
  curleycues, 42
  framing, 42
  patterns, 186, 188, 191
  preparations, 36–40
  problems, 126–127
  stencil cutting, 38
  theorem, 35
  veins, 42
Victorian tray, 64

Wall stencils, 42–46
  patterns, 192, 199
Wax medium, 77, 79–80
White pencil, 88
Wood
  finishes, 86
  graining, 95–96
  preparation, 91
  problems, 130
Worktables, 6

X-acto knife, 24